SEVEN YEARS THAT
CHANGE THE WORLD

1941–1948

THE KOSMON PRESS

LOS ANGELES AND LONDON

1940

---

*A Collection of Prophecies of Yesterday
in the Light of Today
and Tomorrow*

SEVEN YEARS

THAT CHANGE THE WORLD

1941—1948

By

Wing Anderson

CUSTODIAN OF ARCHIVES,
AMERICAN ESSENES OF KOSMON

Author of

THE NEXT NINE YEARS

THE BOOK OF GOLD
152 West 42nd Street
New York, N. Y.

PREFACE TO THE THIRD PRINTING

The original manuscript for SEVEN YEARS THAT CHANGE THE WORLD was received at the book plant on September 9th and the first edition was completed October 31st, 1940. No alterations have been made in the prophecies contained herein since the first printing.

In the months that have passed since the completion of the manuscript several predictions made in this book have become facts and others are well on the way to fulfillment. Franklin Delano Roosevelt was elected to a third term and given dictatorial powers; the United States is at war with Japan; and Germany is meeting defeat in Russia; three prophecies fulfilled in little over a year's time.

Events occur in this mad world with ever increasing speed. No doubt by the time this printing is off the press other predictions contained in this book will have been fulfilled.

It is becoming more difficult with each passing week for the individual to follow the advice given on page 264 for protecting his interests during years of war and inflation. Soon the only avenue to safety will be that road suggested in the concluding paragraph of the book.

THE AUTHOR.

February 1st, 1942.

CONTENTS

ILLUSTRATIONS

FOREWORD

My gran'ther's rule was safer 'n 'tis to crow:
Don't never prophesy—onless ye know.
                    Lowell—"Biglow Papers"

Einstein and the famous Russian, Ouspensky (author of "Tertium Organum") believe that both future and past exist equally . . . that Time is the so-called fourth dimension, an "element in which we are immersed," in which everything is relative and different. Most of us assume that the present moment is the only reality, but these gentlemen—one a scientist, the other an author— say, "No. The present is the most unreal of all, the mere blade of a knife between two endless eternities." A distinction seems to be that we remember some of our past, but cannot "remember" the future.

The future may be likened to a winding road curving over hill and valley, but with short stretches where we sometimes can see what is coming.

Time is but the relation of events in consciousness. Outside of consciousness, Time ceases to exist. The duration of Time is governed entirely by the nature of our own consciousness. In our youth the week preceding Christmas seemed endless. After passing the meridian of life the years seem to fly by with ever-increasing speed, until a year seems like a week. We may wait in a dentist's office with an aching tooth for five minutes and feel that we have waited hours, or we may spend quite a long period of time in some pleasant pursuit and discover the hours have passed like minutes.

There are insects which are born, mature, propagate and die within the space of a day. No doubt their life is as long to them as are three score and ten years to a human being. An insect may experience as many sensations in a life of a day as man does in a century. The measure of time seems entirely dependent on the unit of perception of its percipient.

One concerned with psychic research soon discovers that Time, as we know it, does not exist for those who have passed beyond the limits of our three dimensional environment. The consciousness of the spirit has for its perceptions a far different rate of vibrations than do we in the flesh. This is illustrated in dreams, in which a sequence of events may pass in a few seconds which has seemed, in the dream, to have occupied hours, days or weeks.

Time has an illusory character when judged by human measurements. We are subject to the limitations of our own consciousness, and are slaves to our senses. Time is merely the condition under which our intelligence functions during the years of our life on earth. At death we seem to leave behind the limitations of Time as measured by day and night, spring, summer, fall and winter and adopt a new system of markers for the relation of our experiences.

Past, present, and future, like negative, neutral, and positive are a trinity making one. A cosmic cycle may be similar to a motion picture in that every agent of the cycle is in existence NOW. A motion picture is a complete story. That part before our eyes corresponds to the present, the reels that have been screened represent the past, and the part of the picture awaiting its passage through the projection machine is analogous to the future.

Without a doubt those with prophetic vision are gifted with the ability to catch glimpses of events present in the unseen which time will soon or later bring forth into the seen.

The author has attempted to solve the problem of Time as connected with the prophecies in this book, and to prove by an analysis of today's developments in government, economics and religion that events foretold are upon us. There is no intention to propagandize any system of government or economics, for it is the author's belief that causes were set in motion centuries ago which will culminate in effects that no individual or nation can change. How else could it be possible to foretell the future? If the destiny of nations is a variable, no one could predict centuries ahead the birth of a Hitler, an epidemic of wars, Fascism, revolution and other phenomena of today.

No doubt a few readers will assume that this book is propaganda of the Communists, Fascists, Fifth Column or some other hated "ism," and will write advising the author to leave the country if he doesn't like it. To save such readers their time and stamps, let us assure them that the writer is an American by birth whose forebears on his mother's side were the Wings of Massachusetts, who came to this country about 1670. His father's people came to America from Scotland about 1780. His forebears fought in every war to gain and maintain the independence of our country. His grandfather died from illness contracted while with the Union army of the Civil War.

Wing Anderson is a member of the Masonic and Acacia Fraternities, but is not a member of any Communist, Nazi, Fascist, revolutionary or political party. He has never, at any time, attended any meeting of a Communist or Fascist organization, nor does he intend to. Americans should be able to solve their own problems without advice, instruction or interference from overseas.

As the first republic was born on the American continent, so will also be brought forth on this continent the first true cooperative commonwealth with peace, plenty and security for all. When this new economy comes into existence it will be the product of Americans and not the fruit of either the Third International or the Third Reich.

INTRODUCTION

We are living in "The Time of the End."

The end of the world? The end of civilization? The end of mankind?

No!

The end of unemployment, poverty, starvation, fear. The end of exploitation, imperialism, competition, war. The end of worry, limitation and lack.

A new day is dawning. 'Tis springtime in the Creator's gardens. The "Kingdom on earth as it is in heaven," long prayed for by Christian peoples, is at hand. Look up, for thy redemption from error and sorrow, sickness and death, is nigh.

Down through the centuries many prophets have told of today's events, each sketching a picture which seems to be a segment in a great mural painting of the world today and tomorrow. Every race and nation has had its prophets, each foretelling the future of his people. No time, as we shall find in this book, has produced conditions fitting the pictures sketched by the prophets as do the years 1914 to 1948.

THE NEW DAY

Behold! The New Day cometh;
It breaks atop the hill,
And soon its regal splendor
The world with joy will fill.
Now is the time of changes,
A challenge to our day,
Old systems are collapsing,
New truth is on its way.

All things are being sifted,
The dross is thrown away,
For only that worth saving
Can front the bright New Day.
The day that time has promised,
That truth has sought to bring,
The day the marching ages
And holy prophets sing;
The day of God, the day of Man,
That comes to bless and heal,
And recompense the people
For all the wrongs they feel.
Farewell the day of mammon,
Farewell the day of sin;
Go forth to new found justice,
Let truth its conquests win.
That greatness we shall build us
When man comes to his own,
And all the ills of poverty
And cruel war have flown.
What beauty then shall lead us
To the spirit of our youth,
When all things swing in harmony
With soul expanding truth.
Our hearts shall hold new treasures

And progress proudly run.
To nobleness and glory,
For man, the king of the earth,
Who goes to meet and greet it,
The world's millennial birth.

Transcribed by Samson Greenberg
for Wing Anderson, 1936

CHAPTER I

PROPHECIES OF THE POETS

SONG OF THE SOWER

On the sad earth, as time grows grey,
  When men by deadlier arts shall die,
And deeper darkness blot the sky,
  Above the thundering fray;
And realms that hear the battle cry
  Shall sicken with dismay;
And chieftains to the war shall lead
  Whole nations with the tempest's speed to perish;
In a day.

The above poem was written in 1871 by William Cullen Bryant. Evidently Bryant foresaw the years of war, but was unable to see beyond into the millennium as did Tennyson in 1842 when he wrote "Locksley Hall."

TENNYSON'S PROPHECY

"I dipt into the future, far as human eye could see,
Saw the Vision of the world, and all the wonder that would be;

Saw the heavens fill with commerce, argosies of magic sails,
Pilots of the purple twilight, dropping down with costly bales;

Heard the heavens fill with shouting, and there rain'd a ghastly dew,
From the nations' airy navies grappling in the central blue;

Far along the world-wide whisper of the south wind rushing warm,
With the standards of the people plunging thro' the thunder-storm;

Till the war-drum throbb'd no longer, and the battle-flags were furled
In the Parliament of man, the Federation of the world."

CHAPTER II

PROPHECIES OF ENGLAND

The numerous instances where modern inventions have been foretold in prophecy is truly amazing. Many prophecies agree on world events and most of them concur in predicting changes in topography, climate, religion, governments and economy years ahead.

The War of Armageddon, now in its second phase, has been prophesied in every nation and to every people. Most of the prophecies agree that this war will be tragic beyond description, and will be followed by a wave of revolution. War, pestilence, epidemics, starvation, famine, earthquakes, and appalling natural catastrophies will cause the death of millions. Armageddon and this "Time of Trouble" will purge the world of selfishness and war, and prepare the way for a thousand years of peace and plenty.

England is the home of many prophecies, the best known of which are those of Mother Shipton. This remarkable woman was born in 1486, during the second year of the reign of Henry VII, at a place called Knaresborough, in Yorkshire, England. There are several tales told about her life, but it is doubtful if much of the real truth regarding the woman is known. There is no doubt, however, regarding her prophecies, for many of them were fulfilled during her life and in the centuries since.

The book from which the following prophecies were taken was printed in England in 1864, and is probably a partial copy of a book printed in 1797. The first collection of Mother Shipton's prophecies was published in 1641. A copy of this first edition can be found in the British Museum.

Mother Shipton predicted the discovery of America in 1492, and the gold rush of 1848 in the following:

> In a land that is now unknown
> Gold shall be found and shown.

Another of her prophecies pertaining to America reads:

> Over a wild and stormy sea,
> Shall a noble (Sir Walter Raleigh) sail,
> Who to find, will not fail,
> A new and fair countree,
> From whence he will bring
> A herb (tobacco) and a root (potato)
> That all men shall suit,
> And please both the ploughman and king,
> And let them take no more than measure;
> Both shall have the even pleasure,
> In the belly and the brain.

The reader will recognize our modern inventions predicted in the following:

> Iron in the water shall float,
> As easily as a wooden boat.
> Through hills man shall ride,
> And no horse be at his side.
> Carriages without horses shall go,
> And accidents fill the world with woe,
> Around the world thoughts shall fly,
> In the twinkling of an eye,
> Under water men shall walk,
> Shall ride, shall sleep, shall talk,

3

In the air men shall be seen
In white, in black, in green.
Fire and water shall more wonders do.
England at last shall admit a Jew,
The Jew that was held in scorn
Shall of a Christian be born, and born.

The last three lines of the above are worthy of special attention in relation to the British-Israel movement in England and the U. S. A. This group of over a quarter of a million people in England believe that England is now the home of one of the lost tribes of Israel, and that the English are descended from the Jews.

Mother Shipton seems to have had a clear vision of the present generation, for she prophesied that in a far-off day:

Women will dress like men and trousers wear,
And cut off all their locks of hair.
They will ride astride with brazen brow,
And love shall die, and marriage cease,
And nations wane and babes decrease,
And wives shall fondle cats and dogs,
And men shall live much as hogs,
Just for food and lust.

Mother Shipton placed her prophecies in time by their association with modern inventions. Could she have given a more accurate dating of the World War than by predicting it as coming in the same generation with the motion picture, submarine and airplane?

When pictures look alive, with movements free,
When ships, like fishes, swim beneath the sea,
When men, outstripping birds, can soar the sky,
Then half the world, deep-drenched in blood,
Shall die.

4

Did Mother Shipton foresee Hitler and his "blitz-krieg" of 1940 when she wrote the following?

> An APE shall appear in a leap year,
> That shall put all womankind in fear;
> And Adam's make shall be disputed;
> And Roman faith shall be uprooted,
> And England will turn round.

The following stanzas seem to prophesy a great earthquake or change in the location of the poles of the earth, as foretold in so many prophesies from other sources:

> Waters shall flow where corn doth grow;
> Corn shall grow where water doth flow,
> Houses shall appear in the vales below,
> And covered be by hail and snow.
>
> The time will come, when seas of blood,
> Shall mingle with a greater flood.
>
> Great noise there shall be heard, great shouts and cries,
> And seas shall thunder louder than the skies;
> Then shall three lions fight with three, and bring
> Joy to a people, and honour to the King.
>
> Thunder shall shake the earth;
> Lightning shall rend asunder;
> Water shall fill the earth;
> Fire shall do its work;
> Men shall————he shall——————.

I leave it to the reader to fill in the dashes. Possibly the vision faded.

The following prophecy is as true of the U. S. A. as it is of England:

> Taxes for blood and for war
> Will come to every door.

5

In the following, the first two lines seem to foretell the building and destruction by fire in 1938 of the Crystal Palace in London. Do the last two lines forecast the conquering of England by Germany? The eagle was the symbol of Germany, and the lion remains the insignia of England.

> A house of glass shall come to pass
> In England—but alas!
> War will follow with the work
> In the land of the Pagan and the Turk;
> And State and State in fierce strife
> Will seek each other's life.
> And when the North shall divide the South,
> An Eagle shall build in the Lion's mouth.

Did Mother Shipton predict the bombing of London in the following phrase?

> A river and a town shall be on fire.

No one seems to have been able to make much sense out of this stanza:

> In the KING'S house the POPE shall dwell,
> A Packhan the POPE'S house shall raise,
> Harry shall be nine. Joseph four. Tom a liner.
> Charles two. The Old Man VIII.
> And bitters with and without for all.

Not all of Mother Shipton's prophecies foretold trouble. The following predicts a time of peace and plenty after the wars are over:

> The fiery year as soon as o'er,
> Peace shall then be as before;
> Plenty everywhere be found,
> And men with swords shall plough the ground.
>
> All England's sons that plough the land,
> Shall be seen book in hand.

Learning shall so ebb and flow,
The poor shall most wisdom know.

The following prophecy seems to be seeing its fulfillment at the present time. It is the only prediction in the writer's collection of prophecies by Mother Shipton that pertains to France.

> Three times three shall lovely France
> Be led to dance a bloody dance.
> Before her people shall be free
> Three tyrant rulers shall she see;
> Three times the people rule alone,
> Three times the people's hope is gone;
> Three rulers in succession see,
> Each spring from a different dynasty.
> Then shall the worser fight be done,
> England and France shall be as one.

This prophecy evidently alludes to the battles of Blenheim, Waterloo and the Blitzkrieg of 1940. The rulers are doubtless Louis XVI, Napoleon the First, and Hitler. The revolutions of 1792, 1830 and 1848 have fulfilled part of the prophecy wherein it is said, "Three times the people rule alone; Three times the people's hope is gone," in which phrase all readers of history will recognize the political estrangement and want of constitutional freedom which the people of France have endured by allowing the usurpation of power by the first Napoleon, Louis Philippe and Hitler.

The last two lines of the prediction seem to foretell the conquest of France by Germany under Hitler, and the consolidation of the governments of England and France under the Third Reich.

How is it possible for anyone to dispute the facts of prophecy after reading the auguries of this woman who lived over five hundred years ago? Not only was she able to foretell the discovery of America in 1492, while she was alive, but she also foretold the discovery of gold in California almost a hundred years later. Not only did she foresee the steamboat, telegraph, submarine, automobile, radio and airplane of this generation, but she also evidently foresaw the end of our capitalist economy when she said:

> Fire and water shall wonders do,
> England shall at last admit a foe,
> The end of the world shall come
> In eighteen hundred and eighty-one.

In naming the year 1881, Mother Shipton made the mistake common to many prophets. Others name 1848, 1881, or 1914 as marking the end of competition and the birth of co-operation.

In this book it will be shown that the year 1948 marks the birth of the fourth generation of Kosmon, the generation of builders, just as 1914 marked the birth of the third, or rebel generation, the generation of destroyers. It is the youth born during the war years of 1914–1918 who will tear capitalism apart and replace it with a co-operative commonwealth of nations.

Mother Shipton lived to an extraordinary old age. During her life she was believed to be a witch, yet all who knew or heard of her held her in great esteem.

A stone erected to the memory of Mother Shipton stands near Clifton, about a mile from the city of York, and carries the following epitaph:

> Here lyes she who never ly'd,
> Whose skill often has been try'd;
> Her prophecies shall still survive,
> And ever keep her name alive.

8

CHAPTER III

THE PROPHECIES OF JOANNA SOUTHCOTT

In the year 1750 a woman was born in Devonshire, England, named Joanna Southcott. She may prove to have been England's greatest prophet. During her life she foretold many events by listening to a voice known to her as the Voice of Truth, which she accepted as the voice of God. Although inaudible to others, this voice was as clear to Joanna Southcott as were the voices of her family and friends.

For nine years she wrote down the statements made to her by this voice. Those years brought so many things to pass, as foretold, that her faith in its promptings was established. Thereafter, she published many books and prophecies.

She was told that God had chosen her to be the instrument through which He would warn the world that He would soon set up His kingdom on earth, destroy all evil, and establish a new heaven and earth. She was told that the signs that would precede the setting up of the new kingdom would be:

Nations will rise against nations, and there shall be famines and pestilences and earthquakes in divers places. When these things come to pass, look up, for redemption draweth nigh.

A poem found in Book 44 of her writings, page 35, describes this new heaven to be ushered in following the trying times such as we have today:

Then all mankind must surely know Me,
And judge Me by My powerful reign,
When you My kingdom do obtain
And I begin to reign alone,
And banish Satan from his throne.
For a new earth shall then appear,
Like Eden's garden watered here.
And peace and plenty shall be found,
And every heart in Me be crowned.
And every nation then shall come,
In heart united as one man.
And if that gold can do you good,
I've mines are hid that shall be showed,
And in the seas I've hidden store,
And then I'll bring it all on shore.
And then I'll make all barren lands,
To bring in glorious crops for man:
And every heart I'll fill with love,
And the good fruit they all shall prove.
A perfect knowledge then of Me—
Angels and men shall then agree.
I'll cultivate the barren lands,
And the wild beasts shall silent stand,
And all the earth I'll fill with store.
The storms and tempests shall be o'er;
No burning heat shall then appear,
But pleasant weathers bright and fair.
No searing frosts to chill your blood,
Nor piercing cold as it hath stood,
But summers pleasant, winters mild;
And man in heart I'll so beguile,
That every man shall have a wife,
And love her equal to his life,
And happy offspring shall appear,
For to complete your pleasures here.
This I designed for man at first,
And I'll fulfill it at the last.

10

The following prophecy seems to pertain to the Hitlerian wars and their aftermath, should the people of England still refuse to accept God:

"Because the Famine then they'll fear,
  To see it in the following years,
  If men don't hasty then repent;
  Because My mind is fully bent,
  If England will not turn to Me,
  The Famine they will surely see,
  When I have stopped the raging war,
  For short and sharp it shall now appear.

  The clouds shall gather fast at first,
  That in your land they strong shall burst;
  And if your foes I conquer here,
  It is for those that wish Me here
  Their King and Conqueror for to be,
  Then I must wound their enemy;
  If they invade this very land
  My Sealed People they shall stand,
  I say, to see their foes to fall;
  He cannot come to conquer all,
  Though havoc great I know he'll make,
  But, O My friends shall I forsake?
  No—I will not leave them at that time.
  But now within I know My mind—
  If all these things should so appear,
  The Sword and Plague come in one year,
  Or any fatal like disease,
  So perfect come like My decrees,
  Can unbelief abound in man?
  The truth so plain they must discern;
  With all the truths that are past before:
  Can unbelief in man appear?
  Unto thy thoughts I answer thee,
  The thing is possible to be."

England's warning is repeated in the following poem, which seems to foretell revolution in other countries before it strikes in England:

THE SPIRIT OF TRUTH

"Because the ox his master knows,
  The ass his master's crib,
But Israil backward they do go,
  And do not know their Lord;
The birds know their appointed time
  To build and hatch their young,
But man is wasting all his time,
  Nor knows the days to come,
That like the birds 'tis time to build,
  And make their nest secure;
The hawk is hovering o'er the fields,
  And will your joys devour.
And therefore be not now unwise,
  But seek the truth to know;
I will no longer now disguise
  If men do careless go,
Their houses desolate will be,
  The flames will kindle fast;
In every land My hand you'll see,
  And England's die is cast,
But every land I'll visit first,
  That England may awake.
But here My anger it will burst,
  And make your hearts to shake;
Unless, like thee, they do begin
  To seek their chosen Friend,
And seek to hear the words of Me—
  'Tis deep what thou hast penned.
The grapes have made the nations drunk;
  The children now appear
To end as Noah's sins began;
  Then see the deluge near—
To run with blood, much like the flood.
  Abroad in every land:

'Tis kindling fast, the flames will burst—
Ah! how will England stand
Encompassed round with such a sound
The deluge from abroad!
And now at home doth England groan;
Your sorrows will be known,
Could you discern how I do wain,
Then waining you would take;
If you do not, I'll tell your lot—
Your sorrows they will break."
From "Caution to the Sealed"

The following are some of the prophecies found in her writings seeming to bear directly on the present war between England and the Third Reich:

London will not shun the severe stroke of death and the judgements that are over their heads.

The sea shall be laden with ships and many shall break in pieces.

I promise (1794)* that England shall be defended from the foreign enemy and not invaded.

The Turks shall be utterly destroyed for the sake of the Jews.

As I destroyed the Philistines and Egypt, so will I now destroy the Turks, and their land will I give into the hands of Israel.

Of France and Spain and every distant coast, I'll save a remnant, but one nation lost, and that should be for the sake of the Jews, that I should destroy the nation that has their possessions.

I will establish the throne of David in Jerusalem as I have promised.

Then shall the last day come, that a remnant of those that were cast off (the Jews) must be gathered in and made a strong nation.

Egypt you (England) must first possess.

When earthquakes and famine begin to take place, then know that woe has come upon man.

I told you that it was by war that My kingdom would come in.

* Brackets denote dates prophecies were given, or comments of the author.

All lands in madness everyone shall see.

All nations that forget God will be turned into Hell.

Every land I'll visit first, that England may awake.

The many prophecies of Joanna Southcott, proven true by time, have caused the attention of students of prophecy to be centered on a box of her writings which was sealed during her lifetime (born 1750, died 1825) and removed to London upon her death. Between the years 1801 and 1813, many of her writings were added to the box, which was given into the hands of her followers. This box has been passed on to different custodians during the years since her decease in 1825, and is now in England awaiting the time when the Church of England shall fulfill the conditions set by her for its unsealing.

It was prophesied that the box will be opened at a time of great national danger, in the presence of twenty-four bishops of the Church of England and twenty-four believers in the divine inspiration of Joanna Southcott. It is also said that God will manifest Himself at the opening of the box, and that nothing but the advice given in the prophet's writings can save England from utter ruin.

The bishops sent for the box in February, 1918, but as they refused to abide by the conditions prescribed by Joanna Southcott for the opening, the custodians refused permission to break the seals.

As England will face great danger shortly, we will await the unsealing and publication of Joanna's prophecies with sustained interest.

The second World War between Germany, England,

14

and France was foreseen by many, both before the first World War and immediately after. Lloyd George and H. G. Wells stated in 1918 that another world war was not far away. The former Kaiser of Germany also stated that there would be another great struggle. Abdul Baha, before he passed on, stated at Acca that another general war would stop the trend of materialism and turn people to God. Marshal Foch is said to have shed tears when the armistice was signed, and to have asserted, "This is not the end. We have won the war, but lost peace, and will have it to do over again."

Henry Ford, in an article in the *Los Angeles Examiner*, October 17, 1926, stated, "About five years ago one of the largest manufacturers of munitions in the world, sitting in our offices in Dearborn, said, 'Just wait until the next war. That will be a real war, and it will be a peach.' "

Commenting on this, Mr. Ford remarked, "The man did not seem to be talking sense; but he was very earnest and positive. Now, events seem to be shaping themselves so as to lead to the belief that perhaps this maker of munitions knew exactly what he was talking about."

A munitions manufacturer should know. As soon as the imperialistic nations could raise a new generation of soldiers, twenty-one years after the armistice, we find the armistice ended, the recess over. Is it just a coincidence that Chamberlain and other leading politicians of Britain have investments in the munitions industry?

Before all this is over, the British Empire will have been destroyed. England will remain, but with the destruction of the present financial system she will have lost her power and her colonial possessions.

Oh! England, 'tis thy boasted freedom
    Comes down from an old ancient cry,
It is mine! The world I must conquer,
    It is yours to yield or to die.

While under the broad cloak of freedom
    All banners must needs be unfurled;
Great nations have died like a tyrant
    Attempting to conquer the world.

Old Egypt, the foremost of nations,
    Whose army was great and was brave,
Succumbed to her privileged classes
    And wealth made her labor a slave.

Great Babylon in all of her glory,
    In majesty, grandeur and pride,
Ignored both God and her people,
    In sin and corruption she died.

'Twas Carthage in all of her splendor
    Who gave to her Hannibal fame,
Let greed run away with her reason,
    Leaving only in history a name.

It was Media and Persia united
    Who fattened on Babylon's fall,
Then died when the people had nothing
    When privilege had gathered it all.

When Grecia came on to the carpet
    Under Alexander the Great,
She traded her national glory
    For merely expansion of state.

Then Rome in the pride of her power
    Ruled all in her own bloody way,
She yielded to wealth and corruption
    And finally went into decay.

Oh England, thy hour approaches,
No matter whatever you do,
Thou hast followed the footsteps of others
To the brink of your own Waterloo.
By Lyman E. Stowe. From "What Is Coming." Published
in 1896

CHAPTER IV

Prophecies Concerning Adolf Hitler and Germany

The Hitler Prophecy

You are a spectator of the greatest drama in three thousand years. You are living in the climactic years of a cosmic cycle. You are witnessing the closing scene of the last act of a play which has been on the world stage since the time of man. If you are alive a decade hence, you will see the curtain rise on a *new* world, a better and more happy civilization.

All bibles that have come down to us from the ages past have had one thing in common. In some form, directly stated or implied, the *millennium*—the kingdom of heaven, the theocratic commune, the social commonwealth, or whatever term is applied to a thousand years of peace and plenty—has always been an essential feature of every bible of ancient or modern times.

Where there is such general agreement in sacred books that have commanded the reverence and worship of countless millions in every quarter of the earth, we will find at least a modicum of truth. The preservation of inspired works for thousands of years is evidence of their authority.

The Christian Bible, in common use throughout the Americas and Europe, is fast losing the esteem of the

18

modern youth.   We are becoming a generation of skeptics.   Inspiration commands little respect with the multitude.   Reason is again our idol, as in the days of the French Revolution.   We live in a cycle or period when judgment will be developed.   Sad is the plight of one who has little judgment, or is too lazy to use the talent which he has.   Half the troubles of the world can be attributed to wishful thinking.   It is so much easier to accept as truth the thing we *wish*, rather than that which cold reason tells us must be fact.

However, when evidence is presented which is compelling in its clarity, is it not best to weigh it carefully, even though it may not present a pleasant picture?

It is the intent herein to present evidence that *world conditions of today were foreseen over twenty centuries ago!*

As we look about the world, we find the fulfillment of a prophecy made by the prophet Daniel some time in the second century B.C.

Adolf Hitler, in his rise to power, is a perfect consummation of part of the prophecy of Daniel.   It would seem that the future of this man of destiny is also foretold.   Only the coming years can prove whether this is true.

The writer accepts the King James version of the Bible for what it is: a revision of a revision of a revision of a revision of the Coverdale Bible of 1535.   The Coverdale Bible was based upon the Swiss-German version of 1524, compiled from the Luther, Vulgate, and Tyndale manuscripts.   Recent research and re-translation from the original Aramaic manuscripts by the distinguished Assyrian scholar, Dr. George M. Lamsa, have revealed over *fourteen hundred errors, deletions, and interpolations in the King James version!*

However, these errors and blunders in the Bible should not carry us to the extreme of refusing the good and the truth of the book. We admit the mistakes in inspiration and translation. We accept the fact that the centuries have introduced many changes since the sages, priests, and prophets first inscribed the original manuscripts. Nevertheless, we view what remains in the light of current events, and must admit that the prophecies of the Bible deserve our attention.

We find a description in the book of Daniel that will fit no other man in history as well as Adolf Hitler. That it pertains to our day, who can doubt?

Students of world history agree that we live at the end of an age. Every development in human affairs testifies to a coming change in our civilization. The past ninety-three years have wrought more changes in the world than did the previous twenty centuries. Beginning with 1848, the first year of the present 3000-year cycle, changes have taken place at an ever-accelerating pace. The next seven years will witness even more and greater changes than did the past ninety-three.

We behold the travail period in the evolution of mankind, when the "self" ruled supreme. The next seven years will purge mankind of this old "self," and introduce his true divine selfhood—the super-man, the ensouled man. This man will be a citizen of the super-nation organized for the benefit of the race, and not for the benefit of the politician and "possessing" class only. Man is even now beginning to realize that the self can best be served in the greater self—the community. Man, the individual, will prosper only so far as the community prospers, and the prosperity of the community depends upon the unselfish service of the individual. Self is best served by unselfishness.

The advent of the new order has not come unannounced. In every language, in every country, there are prophecies foretelling the wars of today and the peace of tomorrow.

The interpretation of prophecy is notoriously difficult, and no subject calls forth so many differing opinions. This is not surprising, and, according to revealed writings themselves, many of the prophecies were given in such a form that they could *not* be fully understood until the events foretold reached their fulfillment, and then only by those of open mind, free from prejudice and intolerance.

One of the oldest prophecies pertaining to our present years is that of the prophecy of Daniel, and as it is the one best known to English-speaking people, we will use it for our criterion. At the end of this prophecy, the one to whom the vision of today was given received the following instructions:

But thou, O Daniel, shut up the words and seal the book, even to the time of the end; many shall run to and fro, and knowledge shall be increased . . . and I heard, but I understood not: then said I, "O my Lord, what shall be the end of these things?" And he said, "Go thy way, Daniel, for the words are closed up and sealed till the time of the end" . . .

Daniel XII, 4–10

If it is not intended that even the prophet who received the vision of the world today should know the time with which it dealt, nor be given the inspiration to interpret it, how can one expect to interpret it now without inspiration from the unseen realms from which the original vision was projected? Reason and logic can recognize the accuracy and truth of the prophecy concerned with yesterday, but only spiritual insight can give the interpretation for the part yet unfulfilled.

Examination of prophecies and their many misinterpretations in years past, and the warnings of the prophets themselves, should make us cautious about accepting the speculations of theologians as to their real meanings. On the other hand, the writer being familiar with the various cycles used by the ancients in the formulations of their prophecies, combined with a close study of world politics and economics, and reinforced by a degree of clairsentience,* should be enabled to give an interpretation worthy of the attention of the unprejudiced seeker of light.

Yesterday it would have been impossible to find a man to fit the picture presented in the last chapter of the Book of Daniel. Today we find it a perfect augury of the rise of Adolf Hitler to power. The following eight paragraphs from the last chapter of the Book of Daniel describe the man, his character, his entrance on the world stage, his anti-Semitism, and his god.

ADOLF HITLER, AMBASSADOR OF HELL

1. And in his estate shall stand up a VILE PERSON, to whom they shall not give the honor of the kingdom: but he shall come in peaceably and obtain the kingdom by flatteries.
2. He shall enter peaceably even upon the fattest places of the

---

* E. S. P., or extra-sensory perception. Clear-feeling.

province: and he shall do that which his fathers had not done, nor his fathers' fathers; he shall scatter among them the prey, and spoil, and riches: yea, and he shall forecast devices against the strongholds, even for a time.

3. And he shall stir up his power and his courage against the king of the south (Mussolini) with a great army; and the king of the south shall be stirred up to battle with a great and mighty army; but he shall not stand: for they shall forecast devices against him.

4. And both these kings' hearts (Hitler's and Mussolini's) shall be to do mischief and they shall speak at one table; but it shall not prosper: for yet the end shall be at the time appointed.

5. Then shall he return into his land with great riches: and his heart shall be against the holy covenant, (the House of Israel, or Faithists in the Creator) and the promises made the race: and he shall do exploits and return unto his own land.

6. And the king shall do according to his will: and he shall exalt himself, and magnify himself above every god, and shall prosper till the indignation be accomplished for that which is determined shall be done.

7. Neither shall he regard the god of his fathers nor the desire of women nor regard any god: for he shall magnify himself above all.

8. But in his estate shall he honor the god of forces: and a god whom his fathers knew not shall he honor.

Daniel 11:20

Every change in German government during the past quarter of a century is covered in a few words in this prophecy twenty-two centuries old. Could the exile of the Kaiser, and the rise and fall of the Weimar Republic be more concisely described than in the following:

Then shall he turn his face toward his own land, but he shall stumble and fall and not be found.

Then shall stand up in his estate a raiser of taxes in the glory of the kingdom: but within a few days he shall be destroyed, neither in anger nor in battle.

Daniel 11:19–20

At the termination of the war in 1918, the German Emperor abdicated and fled to Holland. A republic was thereafter declared with Frederich Ebert as its first president. Upon his death, Field Marshal Hindenburg succeeded him.

The Weimar Republic was to be a socialistic democratic government with the objective of establishing in Germany more equitable ownership of the land and the tools of production, a land where plenty should be the lot of all. Only a government has tax-raising power, so verse 20 of the above prophecy refers to the government following the Kaiser.

The kingdom referred to means the kingdom of heaven on earth requested in the Lord's Prayer, wherein every man will enjoy peace and plenty. The Weimar Republic was a feeble attempt to demonstrate government in which every man would be a king. The Republic was destroyed, "not in anger nor in battle," but by persuading senile Paul von Hindenburg to give the Chancellory to Adolf Hitler. When this was done, the destruction of the Republic was assured.

In verse 21, Hitler's rise to power following the destruction of the Republic is announced thus:

And in his estate shall stand up a VILE PERSON, to whom they shall not give the honor of the kingdom: but he shall come in peaceably and obtain the kingdom by flatteries.

"Vile" is defined as synonymous with "morally base, despicable, shamefully wicked, sinful, brutish, and vulgar." Hitler stands convicted by his own words as filling each of these specifications. If a liar is morally base and despicable, Hitler is both of these, for he says in *Mein Kampf:*

24

There is always a factor in a lie that will make it credible. The broad masses of the people fall prey more easily to a big lie than to a small one.

The entire propaganda of Adolf Hitler is built on a foundation of lies. He advocates hate, murder, treachery, brutality, and revolution. Never in the history of government has propaganda been so vile, vulgar, and disgusting as is that of the Third Reich.

Hitler is termed the Fuehrer, the Aggrandizer. He has not been given the honor of the kingdom.

The first attempt made by Hitler to obtain leadership of the German people by force ended in the death of sixteen men and a five-year prison sentence for himself, a term of which he served six months. This defeat convinced him that there was a better way—that of propaganda and flattery, thereby gaining enough votes to elect him to the desired position.

Thereafter, he conceived his fictitious Aryan race, the chosen people of the Lord. He credits the Aryans with every admirable quality, and tells them that "they are the highest humanity which, by the grace of the Almighty, has been given to the world." He pictures them as super-men, and places the Jews at the opposite pole, that he may have someone on whom he can place the blame for all the Aryan troubles. He said to his people, "You would now be rich, powerful, and masters of the world, had not the Jew cheated you of the benefits of your work and sacrifices."

By his unstinted flattery of the German people, he did indeed "obtain the kingdom by flatteries."

2. He shall enter peaceably even upon the fattest places of the province.

As soon as Hitler was made Chancellor, the Reichstag passed an enabling act on March 5, 1933, giving Hitler absolute power and control over all activities in the country: political, economic, industrial, commercial, and cultural. Although never given the title "King," but called "Fuehrer," or "Leader," Adolf Hitler is absolute monarch of all he surveys. Only Aryans, he states, may be citizens of the Reich, and, "Only I alone decide who are Aryans."

In less than a month after Hitler became Chancellor and Reich President, Prussia, Wuttemberg, Saxony, Baden, Schaumberg-Lippe, and Bremen lost their autonomous rights, and became vassals of Hitler. Since then, he has taken Austria and Czechoslovakia without armed resistance. Can anyone deny that Hitler entered peaceably upon the fattest places of the province?

> 3. And he shall stir up his power against the king of the south, and the king of the south shall be stirred up to battle, but he shall not stand, for they shall forecast devices against him.

The king of the south is Mussolini. Mussolini was the first of the Fascist dictators, but he has lost the spotlight since Hitler walked upon the stage. Mussolini and Hitler have, in the past, worked together to propagate Fascism. For some time the Rome-Berlin axis existed, but when Hitler failed in his attempt to take Poland peaceably and war was declared, then the axis weakened. While they were working harmoniously, each to build up his own empire, and co-operating to create world Fascism, Hitler was instrumental in persuading Mussolini to conquer Ethiopia. Both of them backed Franco in the destruction of the Republican gov-

26

ernment of Spain, and its replacement with a Fascist regime was instigated by them.

Shortly thereafter, Mussolini conquered Albania, while Hitler was absorbing Czechoslovakia. At the present time there is considerable feeling in Italy against Hitler and the Germans due to the number of German army officers and members of the Gestapo, or German Secret Police, present in Italy. The anti-German faction in Italy is becoming stronger every day, which fact portends the recovering of power by the monarchy, and loss of power by Mussolini. When Mussolini signed a pact with Hitler, he signed his death decree. Soon Hitler will have Italy and all of its colonies.

> 4. And both these kings' hearts shall be to do mischief and they shall speak at one table; but it shall not prosper for yet the end shall be at the time appointed.

The fact that Hitler and Mussolini have worked with and for each other in obtaining their objectives is well known. Can anyone question that a conspiracy existed between the two to obtain from France and England permission to dismember Czechoslovakia? On September 29, 1938, the infamous Appeasement Agreement was signed at Munich, "at one table," by Hitler, Mussolini, Chamberlain, and Daladier. The first of the following month Czechoslovakia was annexed by Germany, climaxing fifteen days of crisis during which all the great European powers mobilized for war. This annexation has not prospered Germany, for it has been the source of internal friction and has increased the danger of revolution. The cost of the annexation of Czechoslovakia was more than the profit. The end shall be at the time ap-

27

pointed, in 1947, which is the end of the first ninety-nine-year cycle following the birth of the new age in 1848.

At Munich, Hitler stated that Czechoslovakia was all he wanted, and promised England that if she would agree to the annexation, he would make no further demands. Mussolini concurred in Hitler's promises. Both of them lied, for it was Hitler's plan, at the time, to demand Danzig and Poland, as also was it Mussolini's plan to take Albania; also, if circumstances proved favorable, Tunisia from France.

Although these two Fascist dictators apparently obtained their objectives at the council table at Munich, the year 1939 brought on another European war in which Germany, Italy, England and France are still involved. Instead of obtaining Danzig and Poland peaceably, as he did Czechoslovakia, Hitler has destroyed the section of Poland he desired, and lost to the U. S. S. R. the most fertile part. He has started a war two years ahead of the time planned (1941), and is not at all certain of its outcome. That which was spoken at Munich has not prospered.

Hitler, in the year following the Munich conference, took Czechoslovakia and Poland, their resources and national treasuries totaling many millions. In taking Poland, he came into three million dollars belonging to the people of the United States, our country having issued, to Poland, a six million dollar credit through the Export-Import Bank. Lucky were we that only half of this credit had been paid when Hitler marched into Poland.

The "holy covenant" pertains to the holy covenant of

the Bible, wherein Jehovah, creator of heaven and earth, the God of Israel, made the covenant or promise that those who were faithful in their worship of Him, and who did not go running after false gods, would inherit Palestine; would be instrumental in bringing into being the kingdom of heaven on earth, and would provide the spiritual leadership of all peoples.

The Munich Appeasement Agreement was signed on September 29–30, 1938. November 9, six weeks later, witnessed the "Night of the Hatchets"—a night that left the world stunned and appalled at the sadism, brutality, and bestiality of the Nazis. This was an orgy of destruction of Jewish homes, places of business, and other property.

When Hitler came into power in Germany, Jewish wealth totalled about seven billions. Within three months, the Nazis either confiscated or destroyed four and a half billions of this wealth; between eighty and ninety thousand Jews were thrown into concentration camps, an unknown number killed, and ninety thousand fled the country in poverty, not being permitted to take money out of Germany. Jews were driven from the professions, public service, and the universities, and were herded into a Jewish Cultural Organization wherein their professions could only be practiced among themselves.

On this "Night of the Hatchets," five hundred Jewish temples and tabernacles were burned to the ground. In one night, every place of worship was reduced to a pile of smoking ruins. This was the occasion when the Nazis said that Jehovah, the God of the Jews, went "pleit" or bankrupt.

Their homes ruined and plundered, their furniture destroyed, their temples burned, the horror of this night was followed on November 12 by a decree fining the Jews of Germany an indemnity of a billion reichmarks "to pay for reconstruction" of the damage done by the young whelps of the S. S.

The Jews of Germany have been reduced to a poverty stricken, oppressed, homeless, and beaten people. Verily, Hitler's heart is against the holy covenant people.

> 5. And the king shall do according to his will: and he shall exalt himself and magnify himself above every god and shall prosper till the indignation be accomplished, for that that is determined shall be done.

No monarch, past or present, is more absolute than is Adolf Hitler. His word carries life or death to his subjects, as is proven in the several purges within the party. The invasion of Poland, at his command, meant death to many thousands of innocent non-combatants, women and children. At Hitler's command, the Austrian Chancellor, Dr. Dollfuss, was assassinated; his old friends, Ernest Rohm, Schleicher and Gregor Strasser were murdered, besides several cabinet members and a few generals who stood in his way.

Although born and raised a Catholic, he has turned against the "God of his fathers." A year ago, the number of Catholic priests and lay brothers arrested totalled more than eight thousand, and about half of the sixteen thousand members of German monasteries were thrown into jail or concentration camps. Hitler has been proclaimed God of the Third Reich. He will tolerate no equals, not even God Himself, for "the Almighty cre-

ated a favored race, the Aryans, to whom He gave Adolf
Hitler to be their Lord and God." He will have no
competition in the allegiance of the German people, and
makes loyalty to himself a more worthy quality than the
precepts of Christianity.

Hitler is destroying every sect and creed, and intends
to unify the religion of the German people into a new
religion, the worship of Adolf Hitler, God of the Third
Reich, Liquidator of the Jews, Liberator of German
Minorities, Protector of Oppressed Nations. He tells
his people that the babel of religions shall cease when the
world recognizes Adolf Hitler as the new god.

> 6. Neither shall he regard the god of his fathers *nor the desire of
> women*, nor regard any god; for he shall magnify himself
> above all. But in his estate shall he honor the god of forces:
> and a god whom his fathers knew not, shall he honor.

Adolf Hitler has forsaken the god of his fathers for a
new god all his own. Hitler is vice-regent of this god
of force, just as the Pope claims himself to be the vice-
regent of Christ.

Hitler, like Joan of Arc, is clairaudient. He is a
psychic sensitive, and hears with his spiritual ears, as
Daniel saw with his spiritual eyes, the vision quoted in
this prophecy. The world has given birth to thousands
gifted with this spiritual, or psychic, capacity. Every
major prophet throughout the centuries has been born
with a similar sensitivity to the unseen spirit world. Before the present cosmic cycle of three thousand years has
passed, a new sixth race of man will be born with the
spiritual senses and faculties as fully developed as the
physical sight and hearing of the fifth race to which we
belong.

Hitler is a man of destiny just as Joan of Arc was a women destined to save France. He is a man of Uz, a destroyer. He will be followed by men of Es, the builders. *The ground must be cleared and made ready for the builders, and this is Hitler's place in the world today.*

He was foreseen over two thousand years ago. Within the next eight years he will have changed the politics, economics, governments, and religions of the world, for he will have destroyed all present systems.

Edwin C. Hill, in his "Human Side of the News" syndicated in the Hearst papers, is authority for the following:

G. Ward Price, a graduate of Oxford University, has long been a close personal friend of Adolph Hitler. Hitler informed Mr. Price that he was guided by a voice that he alone could hear. This voice had saved his life that he might finish his great mission in Germany. When in a shell-hole with several other men, while a corporal during the war of 1914–18, he heard a voice commanding him to get out and away from the shell-hole. Immediately after he left it, a shell landed where he had been, killing all the other men. This voice has spoken to him many times, he told Mr. Price.

It is more than probable that this voice again saved his life on the night of November 9th, 1939, for he left the beer hall shrine of the Nazis in Munich just ten minutes prior to the explosion of the bomb that killed six charter members of his party.

At every crisis, Hitler departs for his mountain retreat, Berchtesgaden, where he seeks the "silence" to hear the voice of his god. It is not surprising that Hitler should be misled into thinking his god of force is the true god of our planet. Smarter men than he have been fooled, and it is stated in Matthew 24:24 that many false gods shall show great signs and wonders so that even the elect shall be deceived.

Emanuel Swedenborg was one of the greatest scientists the world has known. He was a pioneer on every front of science, and during his life in the eighteenth century was recognized as one of the leading minds of the world. Like Hitler, he was clairaudient and clairvoyant. A minor god of the lower heavens persuaded Swedenborg that he was the Lord, and inspired the writing of many books descriptive of the heavens of the earth.

Joseph Smith received the Book of Mormon subjectively, and the spirit who dictated it told him that he was doing the work of God.

However, there are gods and gods. The Egyptians had scores in their Pantheon. The Catholic Church still recognizes three: the Father, Son and Holy Ghost. The lower heavens of today are full of spirits informing poor deluded mediums that they are Christ, God, Confucius, Shakespeare, Washington, Lincoln, or any other person who commands the respect of men.

Therefore, let us pity Hitler and not blame him for believing that his "guide" is a god, when the truth is that he typifies the antithesis of all the qualities that are attributes of the true God.

Hitler has set aside the Ten Commandments based upon truth, love, brotherhood, equality, gentleness, non-resistance, and replaced them with commandments of his own. For the Ten Commandments of Moses and the Bible, he has substituted seven which might be expressed thus:

1. Thou shalt have no other god than Adolf Hitler.
2. The army and air fleet shall be thy idol.
3. Jehovah, the Architect of the Universe, God of Israel, thou shalt not honor.
4. Thou shalt kill all Jews and Aryan enemies.
5. Thou shalt steal the treasuries and possessions of all conquered peoples.
6. The Jews are the scum of the earth. Hate them.
7. Thou shalt covet all the earth and strive to rule it.

"Mein Kampf" is the new Bible of the Third Reich, a required reading for all Germans. Its author is Adolf Hitler.

"Neither shall he regard the desire of women." What other dictator or king is a bachelor? Mussolini's propensity for women is well-known, as has been that of several of the other dictators. Hitler is probably a celibate and it is not unlikely that he is of neuter sex. It has not been proven that he is homosexual, although homosexuality is rampant throughout the Third Reich. Nor can it be said that he is impotent. If anyone knows the answers, he either will not or dare not tell them. Neither homosexuality nor impotence can be proven, nor is it known that he has ever had intimate relations with women or men. It is probable that on the infrequent occasions when he does show interest in a woman, it is more for political effect than from any personal desire.

The parallel between Adolf Hitler and Joan of Arc is amazing in many ways. Both were psychic sensitives; both clairaudient, guided by a voice inaudible to others; both commanded the armed forces of their countries; so far as is known, neither was interested in the opposite sex; the coming of each was foretold in prophecy, and both were destined to die a death of violence.

Hitler's play upon the world stage has just begun. Three more years will he hold the spotlight. What these three years will do for Adolf Hitler and the world is foretold in prophecy, just as his past has been.

The items from the Book of Daniel seem, without question, to refer to Adolf Hitler, for no other man in history fits the picture presented as does this man.

The Book of Daniel is an odd book in the Bible, for this book, at least in its present form, belongs to the second century B.C., while the other books of the Old Testament had been accepted as canonical almost two centuries earlier, or about 400 B.C. when Ezra read them before the people.

The Book of Daniel is a prophetic book and ties in closely with the books of Revelation, Isaiah, and Matthew. For an interpretation of the future, we must not only consider Daniel in relation to the other books mentioned, but must also consult the archives of the Essenes for an understanding of many of the terms used in these old manuscripts. The Essene writings are vital for use as a key to the cosmic cycles used by Biblical prophets in their allegories.

Prophecies of Germany

The advent of Adolf Hitler upon the European scene has been foretold in many prophecies. A group of these prophecies was collected and published in 1914 in a book entitled "Phophecies and Omens of the Great War." Ralph Shirley, the editor, fell into the same mistake made by most other interpreters of prophecy, in assuming the first section of the War of Armageddon to be the event foretold, rather than the Hitlerian wars of the present.

The most amazing of these prophecies is one found in a book entitled "Derniers Mots des Propheties." This prophecy originated about the year 1600, and was given by a monk called Brother John.

The Antichrist *

The real antichrist will be a German monarch, who will invoke God and give himself out as his messenger.

This prince of lies will represent himself as the arm of the Most High, sent to chastise corrupt peoples.

For several years he will act by craft and strategy. His spies will over-run the earth and will reveal to him the secrets of the mighty.

He will have men in his pay who will maintain, and undertake to prove, his celestial mission.

A war will furnish him with the opportunity of throwing off the mask. After two weeks the world will recognize that the war he originated against the French nation is of universal character.

Not only all Christian and all Mohammedans, but other more distant peoples will be involved. Armies will be enrolled from the four quarters of the globe.

By the third week, the angels will have opened the minds of men who will perceive that this man is the personification of evil, and that they will all become his slaves if they do not destroy this conqueror.

Antichrist will be recognized by these tokens: He will massacre the priests, the monks, the women, the children and the aged. He will show no mercy, but will pass torch in hand, like the barbarians of old. His words will be those of a Christian, but his actions will

---

* Antichrist, according to the Bible, is to be a great enthroned antagonist, who precedes the second coming of Christ and is said to be Evil personified.

resemble those of Nero and of the Roman persecutors. He will have an eagle in his arms, and there will be an eagle also in the arms of his confederate, another monarch.

The latter will be a Christian, and will die from the malediction of the Pope, who will be elected at the commencement of the reign of evil.

Priests and monks will no longer confess and absolve the combatants, for they will be fighting. The Pope will proclaim that those who die fighting will rest in a state of grace, and will ascend to heaven like the martyrs.

The Bull which will proclaim these things will create a great sensation. It will revive the courage of the foes of Antichrist and cause the death of the monarch who is his ally.

In order to conquer Antichrist, it will be necessary to kill more men than Rome has ever contained. It will take the combined efforts of all his antagonists, because France,* England and Russia will not be able to make an end of Germany without the aid of the prayers of all the human race.

Never will humanity have been faced with such a peril, because Antichrist will have become a demon, which will have taken possession of his personality.

Towards the year 2000, Antichrist will be made manifest. His armies will include millions. There will be Christians among his cohorts, and there will be Mohammedans and heathens among his antagonists.

There will not be in the whole world a single spot that is not red. Heaven and earth, water and air, will be red, for blood will flow in the four elements at once.

Germany will hurl itself upon France, which would soon be exhausted but for the aid of England. Germany will make a surprise attack on France, and will invade the land. Germany will find itself forced to relinquish its hold upon France in order to fight Russia, whereupon France, in giving aid to Russia, will pursue the Antichrist into his own land.

* In the original prophecy, the cock, the leopard, and the white eagle are used as symbols for France, England and Russia.

The battles fought up to that time will be as nothing compared to those which will take place in the country of the Third Reich, for the seven angels will simultaneously pour out the fire of their censers upon the impious land.

When the beast finds himself lost he will become furious. It will be necessary for some months that Russia, England and France use their utmost energies in the destruction of the beast.

Men will be able to cross rivers dry shod, walking on the dead, which in places will change the courses of streams. Bodies will be too numerous to bury, for starvation and pestilence will add to the carnage of the battle fields.

Antichrist will sue for peace many times, but the seven angels who march before the three allies will have proclaimed that victory shall not be given except on condition that Antichrist be destroyed.

Russia, England and France will not be permitted to cease fighting so long as Antichrist has soldiers. It will be apparent that the combat, fought where Antichrist forges his arms, is no human conflict.

The three allies will exterminate the last army of the beast. The field of battle will be made into a funeral pyre for the corpses will have altered the features of the land by forming ranges of little hills.

The beast will lose his authority and die in solitude and madness. His empire will be divided into states.

Russia will drive the Mohammedans out of Europe, then will commence an era of peace and prosperity for the world. Each nation will be governed according to its own desires, and will live in peace with every other nation.

Happy will be those who, escaping the terrors of this marvelous time, are able to taste of its fruit.

The foregoing prophecy is remarkable in its description of Hitler, and in the prediction that the Third Reich will meet defeat at the hands of the U. S. S. R.

Several prophecies predict the destruction of Turkey. One such is that originating with a Russian monk, Thosmas, born in the year 1778:

38

When the allied kings march on Constantinople (now Istambul), sufficient blood will flow for a lamb to swim. The Turks will be divided into three parts. The first will perish in the war, the second will retire to Asia, and the third will remain in Europe. No one who hears me now will see this, but their children may.

"Germany to Be Destroyed"

In the year 1872, a book was published entitled "Voix Prophetiques, ou Signes, Apparitions et Predictions Modernes," containing a remarkable prophecy covering the first and second sessions of the European war. This prophecy was given by the Cure d'Ars, Father Vianney, who died in 1859. The Cure is said to have foretold the first war, and prophesied that a second war would follow after a certain lapse of time. In regard to this latter war, he said:

The enemy will not go immediately. They will again return and destroy as they come. Effective resistance will not be made. They will be allowed to advance, and after that their supplies will be cut off and they will suffer great loss. They will retreat towards their own country. They will be followed, and few will reach their goal. Then all that they have taken away will be restored and much more in addition.

Prior to the first World War, there lived in France a Madame de Thebes, who was the most famous clair-voyante in her country. Each year she published an almanac, under her own name, containing predictions covering the coming year. One of the most remarkable of her predictions is found in her 1912 almanac:

Germany menaces Europe in general and France in particular. When the war breaks out, hers will be the responsibility, but after the war there will be no longer either Hohenzollern or Prussian hegemony. This is all Berlin will gain by her violence and the brutality of her political methods. I have said, and I repeat, that the days of the Emperor are numbered, and after him all will be changed in Germany. I say the years of his reign, I do not say the years of his life.

Two distinct visions pursue me. I see a Germany which is torn asunder, South against South, North against North. It is the revolutionary movement, popular fury against the military aristocracy. And at the same time, in spite of all these troubles, resistance continues or at least endeavors to continue, parodying the France of the past, even to its great Revolution. Hostages, massacres, trials, scaffolds, all are there, and, in spite of all this, the enemy has crossed the frontiers. The other vision, more to be feared perhaps, shows Germany ready to give in at once, ready to declare herself conquered, to accept the conditions of the victors, and thus gain time to renew her attacks upon her enemies with greater energy. But in either case there is no more Hohenzollern. Meanwhile, where is the man whose presence I sense, whose coming I foretold last year, and who is destined to arise in Germany in order to make a voice heard which will dominate all other voices, and which will save his unhappy country a part, at least, of the just punishment which Providence reserves for her?

Another prophecy of like kind is that made by Heinrich Heine in his book on the religion and philosophy of Germany. In this, he evidently foresaw the rise of Hitler, the destruction of the Christian Church in Germany, and revival of the old pagan gods:

Christianity has moderated the brutishness of the Germanic races who fought for the mere love of battle. When the cross of Christianity is broken, the long smouldering ferocity of ancient warriors will again blaze up. The Christian Talisman is rotten with decay and will soon crumble and fall. Then the ancient gods will rub the dust of a thousand years from their eyes and will arise from dismantled ruins. Then Thor, with his colossal hammer, will leap up and break into a thousand fragments the Gothic cathedrals. A drama will be enacted in Germany that will make the French revolution seem a harmless idyll.

Another prophecy by this great German poet, a Jew by birth, is interpreted from an article written by Heine in June, 1842.

40

When revolution begins to sweep the earth, we shall see the emergence of the most appalling of all the antagonists who ever stood forth to do battle against the existing order. This antagonist has not as yet made its appearance, but will emerge under the term "Fascism," and will be the most redoubtable adversary who has ever marched against the existing order.

War will be merely the first act of the great drama and will be no more than a prologue. The second act will be the European revolution, the world revolution, the immense combat between the "have-nots" and the "haves."

The future speaks to us of scourges, of blood, of godlessness, and of a great deal of conniving and conspiracy. I advise our grandchildren to come into the world with well padded shoulders and backs.

It may be that the old tradition of absolutism (dictatorship) will step forth once more upon the stage of the world, this time in a new costume, with new slogans and new catchwords.

Heine cast his characters and arranged his props perfectly for the scene today. Fear of revolution stalks every government in the world. Who can doubt but that World War will be followed by the world revolution predicted by many prophecies of the nineteenth and earlier centuries.

THE PROPHECY OF SAINTE ODILE

One of the most remarkable prophecies pertaining to Adolf Hitler and the wars of the Third Reich is the following. This prophecy originated in the seventh century and was embodied in a letter to the brother of Sainte Odile, a Catholic nun, patron saint of Alsace.

It foretells the birth in the valley of the Danube where Hitler was born of a conqueror whose conquests will be world-wide. It predicts a war divided into three periods of eighteen months, nine months and probably four months' duration, and the final invasion of Germany from all sides culminating in the destruction of Hitler. Her prediction concurs with the conclusions of the author in foretelling the finale of Hitler about 1943.

The original prophecy was in Latin. A translation into French was published in 1917 and appeared in the Almanac of the People, a copy of which may be found in the Library Beauchemin. The English version was translated from a reprint of the prophecy which appeared in a French language newspaper of Montreal, Canada, dated May 4th, 1940.

Like many prophecies, the time with which it is concerned was unknown to the seer to whom the vision was given. It seems a common error among seers and prophets to assume that a vision or prophecy pertains to the immediate future when, in fact, it may deal with events centuries ahead.

Listen, listen, my brother—as I have seen the terrors of the forests and mountains, fear has gripped all the people, and never, in any part of the universe, has been such chaos. The time has come when Germany will be called the nation most bellicose of all the earth. The time has arrived when from the bosom of this country has come the terrible warrior who will undertake to spread war over the world. Men under arms will call him anti-Christ. He will be cursed by the millions that will lament like Rachael upon the fate of their children, and will refuse any consolation, because their children will be gone and all will be devastated in their homes.

The Conqueror will come out from the bosom of the Danube and will become a remarkable chief among men. The war that he will wage will be the most terrifying that men have undertaken. His weapon will be fire, and the spears of the soldiers will have points like torches. It will be impossible to calculate the number of cruelties.

He will gain victories on earth, seas, and even in the air, because they will see winged soldiers in incredible attacks—arising to the skies and throwing stars (bombs) down over the cities of the universe. There shall be gigantic fires. The nations will be astonished and will ask where does his power come from? How was he capable of undertaking such a war?

The earth will tremble from the shock of the combats. The rivers will flow red and the sea monsters will be dispersed with terror to the tops of the oceans, while black tempest will spread desolation over all.

The future generations will be astonished that these powerful enemies have not been able to erase the suffering. The war will be long. The Conqueror will attain triumph toward the middle of the sixth month of the second year of the hostilities, and this will end the first period of the bloody victories.

He will say, "Accept my domination!", while continuing his victories, but his enemies will not submit, and the war will continue and he will shout, "Their misfortunes will make them fall, for I am the Conqueror."

The second part of the war will be equal in length to half of the first, and will be called "the period of diminuation." It will be full of surprises and will make the earth tremble. Twenty belligerent nations will fight. Towards the middle of the war the small nations will cry, "Give us peace! Give us peace!" But there won't be peace for those nations. It will not be the end of war for them, but the beginning, for in the end there will be body-to-body fighting in the City of Cities (Rome), and it will be then that we shall see a revolt among the women, who will want to stone him. We shall also see great events in the Orient.

The third period is most brief, and the Conqueror will have lost the confidence of his soldiers. This period will be called the "period of invasion for just retribution." The soil of the Conqueror, due to his injustice and atheism, will be invaded from all parts and plundered. Around the mountains torrents of blood will flow.

Then will be the last battles. The nations will sing hymns of gratitude in the temples of God, and will thank the Almighty for deliverance.

It will be then that a warrior will appear who will disperse the troops of the Conqueror, whose armies will be annihilated by disease unknown and terrible. The soldiers will be discouraged, while the nations will say, "The finger of God is there. It is a just punishment." The people will believe that the end is near. The sceptre will change hands, and my people will rejoice because God is just, although He permits, at times, these depredations and cruelties. The people will regain confidence in God, but they cannot regain the children and women. They shall have something even greater as a recompense. Innumerable regions will be fired and be bloodied, but will be saved in a Providencial way by herioc defenders. The region of Paris will be saved because of its mountains, which are blessed, and because of its religious people. All this will happen when everyone believes she is condemned to disappear.

Then the people will go to the mountains and thank God because the men have seen such abominations in this war that their generation will never want to see another war. There shall be misery. Meanwhile, in these days, the people will not fear any more the anti-Christ, for he can only father those that crime does not frighten. He will give life to new killers and there shall be more tears shed.

But the era of peace will arrive under the seal as two crescents of the moon united under the peer of the cross,* because in these days, men frightened will adore God in truth, and the sun shall again shine brightly.

THE PROPHECIES OF MICHEL NOSTRADAMUS
(1503–1566)

No collection of prophecies could be complete without a few lines from those of Michel De Nostradamus, the most famous prophet that ever appeared in Europe. This sixteenth century astrologer predicted the French Revolution, Napoleon's career, the outbreak of the first World War, the abdication of King Edward the Eighth, the Spanish Civil War, the present European war, and the fate of Hitler.

Michel De Nostradamus was born of Jewish parents at Saint Remy en Provence in France in 1503. From his grandfather he inherited ancient manuscripts of the tribe of Issacbar, which had been brought out of Egypt at the time of the exodus. After assimilating the information contained in the manuscripts, he burned them for reasons best known to himself.

* This phrase may signify the signature of the All Highest Creator.

44

Nostradamus was prophet and physician to Charles IX of France. During his life he held a well earned reputation as a man of profound wisdom and a prophet of amazing skill and accuracy. While now a legendary figure, we still have early editions of his prophecies, which passing years have proven accurate time and again. The most famous of his prophecies are contained in his manuscripts entitled "The Centuries," in which he prophesies cardinal events from the sixteenth to the end of the twentieth century.

"The Centuries" include prophecies for all history, but a prophecy concerned more with religious, political and geological crises, beginning in 1792 and ending in 2000, is the one entitled "L'Epitre á Henri II." The following prophecies and their interpretations are taken from both "The Centuries" and "L'Epitre á Henri II":

> Crier Victoire du grand Selin Croissant
> Par les Romains sera l'Aigle clamé
> Ticcin, Millan. Genes y consent,
> Puis par eux-mêmes Basil grand réclamé.

(Trans.) After the Ethiopian victory, Rome will proclaim the Empire at Milan, in Tuscany. King Victor Emmanuel (Duc de Genes) will consent to it. But soon she will call for help to the great king. (Ed: It was at Milan, after the conquest of Ethiopia, that Mussolini proclaimed the Italian Empire and gave Victor Emmanuel the title of Emperor.)

A terrible Italian revolution is predicted in the following:

> Par grand discord la trombe tremblera,
> Accord rompu, dressant la teste du ciel,
> Bouche sanglante dans le sang nagera,
> Au fol sa face oingte de laict et miel.

45

(Trans.) In the Adriatic, great discord will develop, and those who provoke war will perish in blood; while revolutionaries will suffer least.

The next stanza predicts a great slaughter of priests:

> Des gens d'Eglise sang sera espanché.
> Comme de l'eau en si grand abondance,
> Et d'un longtemps ne sera restanché.
> Vae, vae, au clerc, rugne et doléance.

(Trans.) The blood of the people of the church will be spilt like water in great abundance, and for a long time it will not be staunched. Woe, woe, to the clerics, ruin and grief.

War will be general by this time in western Europe.

> L'horrible guerre, qu'en Occident s'appreste
> L'an ensuivant viendra la pestilence,
> Si fort terrible que jeune vieil, et beste
> Sang, feu, Mercure, Mars, Jupiter en France.

(Trans.) A horrible war, for which Europe will prepare. The year following, there will be a plague so strong and terrible that young, old and animals will suffer. Blood, fire, Mercury, Mars, Jupiter in France.

The abdication of Edward VIII, brought about by his love of a woman, was foretold in the following:

> Pour ne vouloir consentir au divorce
> Qui puis apres sera cognen indigne
> Le roi del Isles sera chasse par force
> Mis a son lieu qui de roi n'aura signe.

The prediction also states that the monarchy will be followed by a republic.

Nostradamus' system of calculation differed from popular methods of today. The system used by him seems to be related to the esoteric cosmogony of the builders of the Great Pyramid of Gizeh. Nostradamus called his chart the "Grand Romain" or "Great Roman." The coffin-shaped figure represents the "Sepulcher of the Great Roman," and is formed by drawing lines from the vowels in the Latin words "Floram patere." These two six letter words are spaced around the twelve lines of the zodiac, as shown in the accompanying chart. By use of this formula in connection with his knowledge of astrology, Nostradamus was reputed to have worked out his predictions.

An interpretation of one of his quatrains is said to have Hitler worried. This prediction states that in the year 1944 Hitler will be put in an iron cage and his em-

ZODIAC OF MICHEL DE NOSTRADAMUS
with the
SEPULCHER OF THE GREAT ROMAN

pire destroyed. Nostradamus' prophecy of this event seems to concur with that of Saint Odile, which also foretells the end of Hitler around the year 1944.

THE ANTICHRIST

The term "antichrist" appears in many prophecies. Let us determine what this word means. In the New Testament, the personality of Christ is used to exemplify spiritual wisdom. He taught the lasting benefits of a policy of non-resistance to evil. He lived, as well as taught, his sermons on humility, love, brotherhood, peace and cooperation. He kept himself free of bondage to materialism and the false values of his time. If, then, the term "Christ" stands for tolerance, love, brotherhood, peace and cooperation, any person, organization or nation living by opposite standards may be termed false or antichrist.

Christ was a Hebrew, an Israelite, as were all of the Biblical prophets. The aggressiveness which characterizes the modern peoples does not spring from the Semitic, but from the Aryan branches of mankind. The ancient Hebrews were seldom engaged in strife, and then only as the result of being attacked, and never from any effort on their part at conquest of other peoples.

The Hebrews have always been monotheistic, worshipping one god only—Jehovah, the Creator. The Aryans, with the growth of the Christian religion, have worshipped several gods, have been competitive, aggressive, imperialistic, and frequently engaged in wars of conquest. They have had a multiplicity of gods, the Father, Son, Holy Ghost, Virgin Mary, and the Devil, and have often attributed more power to the devil than to all their other gods combined.

Their faith has not been in the peaceful tenets of Christ, but in their soldiers, their armaments and their material wealth.

Christ is reputed to have said, "I come not to bring peace but a sword." Evidently he foresaw the time when a church would be named after him that would be false to everything he taught, and nations called Christian would be engaged in the War of Armageddon foretold by Hebrew prophets long before his time.

Adolf Hitler seems to personify every tenet antagonistic to peace, love, brotherhood and cooperation, thereby becoming the embodiment of Antichrist.

The result of the reign of this Antichrist is related in Revelation 13:5–17 and Isaiah 14:16–17, "He will lay the entire world in ruins and destroy the cities thereof." He is truly the Ambassador of Hell, if we accept hell as meaning chaos, disintegration, confusion, strife, hate, and death, the antithesis of heaven signifying harmony, organization, peace, love and life.

There are seven things that may be said of the War of Armageddon * that may not be said of any other war:

1. The number of nations and men engaged will surpass that of any other war in history.
2. Battles will last for days, weeks and months.
3. Babylon will be destroyed. Babylon, in the terminology of Biblical prophecy means the international banking system ruling all nations.
4. Wars, famines, pestilences and bestiality will increase as property and men waste away. The war of 1914–1918 saw no such wanton murder of noncombatants as is now taking place, nor did Europe see any such rape and needless killing as Ethiopia, China, Poland, Belgium, the Netherlands, France and England have witnessed. The "four sore judgements" on godless, unbelieving, self-righteous Christendom will result in the overthrow of the competitive system and the formation of a world community of nations. The only things that capitalistic, Christian nations will unite for, at present, are war, suffering and death.
5. The conflict in Europe is being waged among so-called Christians. *Christendom is being shot out of existence.*

* The term "War of Armageddon" means not only the great war of 1914–1918 but all international wars throughout the world during the 33 year cycle from 1914 to 1948 spoken of in the Bible as the "Time of Trouble."

6. War is being waged not only on the earth, but on the sea, under the sea, and in the air.

7. Christian nations are more warlike than those of any other religion. Mohammedans seldom make war on Mohammedans, nor Buddhists on Buddhists, nor Brahmans on Brahmans, but Christian nations have always been warring on one another. "I come not to bring peace, but a sword" is a prophecy fulfilled.

The first World War was stated to be a "war to end war" a "war to make the world safe for democracy." The nations are having a hard time finding a slogan with which to fool the people as an excuse for a second world war. The true explanation is that the rulers of Christian nations are determined to prevent the peace and plenty awaiting all mankind when a cooperative instead of a competitive economic and governmental system is adopted by the nations. The Pope makes this clear in his call for the nations to combine that Communism may be destroyed. And the Nazarene was a Communist, born and raised in an Essene community where all property was collectively owned, where there were no wealthy or poverty stricken classes, but peace and plenty were enjoyed by all. Verily, Christianity has wandered a long way in twenty centuries.

Time and space will not permit giving the Biblical quotations and their interpretations for our authority, but we will summarize the future of Hitler in the following predictions.

A second League of Nations will be formed in a short time consisting of the seven dominant nations of Europe. A money system will be adopted for use throughout the league.

A peace will be signed with the Jews, who will be returned in greater numbers to Palestine. This peace will be terminated at the end of three and a half years, when they will undergo the great tribulation. Two-thirds of the Jews in Palestine will be killed and the remainder will "seek Jehovah, their God, and David, their King."

Hitler will make peace with Rome, and the Pope will work with Hitler in making the Roman Catholic Church supreme. It is interesting, at this time, to call to the reader's attention that the number of the Beast of Revelation is 666—the number of Rome.

Interpretation of 666

Latin motto on Pope's crown—Vicarius Filii Dei. Latin letters are numerals as well as letters. Giving such letters in this motto the numerical meaning, we have:

V—5	F	D—500
I—1	I—1	E
C—100	L—50	I—1
A	I—1	___
R	I—1	501
I—1	___	
U—5	53	
S		
___		
112		

VICARIUS—112
FILII   — 53
DEI   —501
    ___
    666

"And he causeth all, both small and great, rich and poor, free and bond, to receive a mark in their right hand, or in their foreheads. . . . Here is wisdom. Let him that hath understanding count the number of the beast; for it is the number of a man, and his number is six hundred, three score and six."

Revelation, Chap. 13: 16–18

Catholics cross themselves on their foreheads, and in Latin countries they also cross their palms.

51

Capitalism and Rome are blood brothers, and will work together to maintain the competitive capitalistic system of private profit and control of the land and resources of the world by a few rather than by all mankind as the Creator intends they shall be.

Does it seem impossible that Rome should again rule the world as she did centuries ago? It was in 1914 that the writer first heard of the prophecies of the Seven Day Adventists foretelling the recovery of temporal power by the church, and of a time when she would again rule the nations. In 1929 the State of Vatican City was recognized by the nations of the world, and in the opening days of 1940, Franklin D. Roosevelt appointed Myron Taylor as his personal ambassador and the representative of the United States at the Papal State. This was an opening wedge that may lead to a permanent United States ambassador at the Vatican. Catholic power is gaining day by day in the United States.

Before Christianity destroys itself, Rome will again have her day as ruler of the world.

This gain has been continuous since 1789. At that time the Catholic Church had only 25,000 adherents in the United States, shepherded by but thirty priests. To-day the Catholic Church claims 20,000,000 followers in the U. S. and 30,000 priests. From poverty, in the early days in America, she has grown to an institution holding title to property valued at over two billion, most of it free from taxes. From a scattered flock she has developed into an organization of great political power.

The holdings of the Catholic Church in the U. S. are not by any means confined to real estate, churches, and schools. Ferdinand Lundberg in 1936 compiled from the N. Y. State Banking Department the following list of corporations in which the Church holds investments: The Baltimore and Ohio, General Motors, U. S. Steel, Du Pont, Pure Oil, Commonwealth Edison, Goodyear Rubber, Douglas Aircraft. These are but a few of the corporations in which the Church has interests.

A similar condition exists in every other country where the Catholic Church is entrenched, and largely explains the Pope's stand against communism and his support of capitalism and all its evils.

How can the Church preach pacifism so long as it draws income from the merchants of death? How can it advocate plenty for all when its power and property depend on the maintenance of the system that has given it power and wealth?

The Church prays for peace, but invests its funds in companies whose income is largely derived from the manufacture of the instruments of death.

Is not the Church itself antichrist; is it not the false Christ of prophecy? The Nazarene was a Communist born in a community of the Essenes * where all property was held in common. Instead of the power of wealth, the Nazarene's power was the power of truth.

---

* The Essenes were custodians in Egypt of the ancient wisdom first given to humanity through Zarathustra of Persia nine thousand years ago. The initiations and system of life of this ancient order appeared in every quarter of the globe in the early days of every three thousand year cycle. While the old nations are destroying themselves by war, the prophets developed by this school lead a few of the spiritually enlightened from crashing civilization to pioneer a new order of life. Chine, for whom China is named, Brahma, Confucius, Abraham, Moses, Joshu (the Nazarene), and Eawatah (Hiawatha) were all masters and prophets of the fraternity.

Essene is pronounced "Es" as in "esquire," "sene" as in "seen." It means of the spirit, or non-resistant, peaceloving.

The only riches of the man whom the Church claims to represent were the clothes he wore. Not alone the Church of Rome, but all its offspring; the Church of England, the many protestant creeds, the churches of America, are all more or less false to every tenet he gave.

Anything that is counterfeit is false. Any person or organization that preaches one thing and acts another is false to the thing it claims to be. If the word "Christ" means truth, love, brotherhood, then our present day capitalistically-dominated Christian churches are false Christs, for they do not teach truth nor *practice* love and brotherhood. They may preach such things, but they hypocritically close their doors to the ill-clad and poor, and welcome the rich and men of war. The church will generally be found on the side of the reactionaries, lining up in support of any group trying to prevent a more abundant life.

By mentioning these facts, we do not mean to condemn the churches. Every religion, every church, and every school of thought has a part in the education and unfoldment of man. "All roads led to Rome." So do all religions lead to heaven. Those who worship one god only, the Creator, are on the short path, the positive road. Those who worship a savior or other gods are on the long or negative path. One is as essential as the other. Since the first race came on earth there have been three types of religion: the *materialist*, whose god is the world, the *spiritualist* whose gods are of the lower heavens and the Essene Faithist, or Israelite, who goes to the source of life and has faith in his creator only. Each is a part of the eternal trinity. Some are born to one path, some to another, but all religions are instruments of the Father and all churches lead, eventually, to Him.

If you can not accept the dogma of the Christian Church, don't worry, for you are in good company. George Washington, Abraham Lincoln, Thomas Jefferson, Walt Whitman, Thomas Paine, and countless others could not confine their thinking to the limits set by the churches. Each of these men recognized the authority of a supreme intelligence and were, to a greater or lesser degree, faithists in the Architect of the Universe, the Great Spirit, The All ONE, the I AM, Jehovah, or any name you care to give to the source of life. These men recognized the fact that the universe is governed by the law of cause and effect, eternal justice. They did not feel the need or desire for a savior upon whom to throw the burden of their mistakes. Every great prophet has taught that one reaps what one sows, and every mistake (call it sin if you will) brings its own punishment. Those who think that priest, Christ, or savior can nullify the law of compensation are but fooling themselves.

The Faithist, Christian, Mohammedan, Buddhist, or Bushman are all in the same category. We are all sons and daughters of the same father (Jehovah) and mother (earth), but are attending different schools. After the destruction of every religion that recognizes any other god than the Creator, we will have unity in government and economics the same as we will have it in religion. Then will the brotherhood of man be a fact and not a fantasy.

But first mankind must go through the experience of worshipping many false gods. A god of force will appeal to a Fascist far more than will a god of peace. The Jews find money a more acceptable idol for worship than Jehovah, and Christian nations have more faith in their armies and navies, emblems of their god of war, than they have ever had in the god of Christ. This multiplicity of gods will cause such chaos upon earth and such spiritual indigestion that mankind will spew them all out, as did Russia. Then and then only will we be ready to recognize the fatherhood of the Creator (the I AM that I AM), the motherhood of the earth and the brotherhood of man.

Do you not think the Creator * knew what He was doing when He caused the founders of our country to provide religious liberty and prohibit ANY religion to be enforced by the state? Say what you will of the

---

* The Old Testament was written four hundred years after the death of Moses, and is a conglomeration of the histories of Israelites and Egyptians. The terms Jehovah, God, Lord God and Lord became confused and their true meaning lost in the years since Moses lived.

When used correctly, the term Jehovah is the name of the Creator, the I AM THAT I AM, the Great Spirit, Architect of the Universe, the All One, the Supreme Intelligence or First Cause Who holds within His Own Being all creation.

There is but one Jehovah, but there are many gods, lord gods and lords. Each planet has but one god, several lord gods and many lords. Jehovah is a name, the others are titles.

God is the chief executive of our planet.

A Lord God is governor over a specific area and the heavens above it.

A Lord is governor over a section of the earth's area and the people living on it.

All TRUE lord gods, lords and God inspire both corporeans and spirits to worship the Creator.

All FALSE gods inspire corporeans and spirits to worship either themselves or another individual spirit.

The lower heavens are filled with counterfeit, false and fictitious gods and lords who are self appointed and without truth or authority. Readers interested in psychic research, or who have investigated mediums to any extent, are well aware that spirits will take unto themselves any name or title that inspires reverence and respect.

A pseudo-religious-patriotic cult has recently established branches in many cities having Sainte Germaine as their idol-in-chief with Christ his lieutenant.

U. S. S. R., the fact remains that it is the only country that is willing to concede God the ability to look out for Himself. All other countries of Europe attempt to be self-appointed sheriffs for Him.

Church, state, and finance are all good and have their work to do, but when they combine to rule the world, they become a trinity of hell.

The Church has always prayed for the victims it was about to murder, and quoted the gentle sayings of Jesus as it sent millions to the rack, the fire, and the sword. It has praised poverty as it sought wealth; boasted of itself as the caretaker of civilization while it conspired to keep its followers steeped in ignorance and superstition.

The state and church have always, sooner or later, become partners in exploiting the people. The manuscripts in the archives of the Essenes have this to say of the government:

In ancient times, governments and laws were provided for nations and peoples. Government should be as a father over the people and not as a separate matter against them. But government becomes one thing and the people another. That which should be one entity has been made into two.

Governments have become separate selves from the people; and the people are as servants, supporting the lawmakers who trade in projects and schemes for their own profit and glory.

Since the earliest days, all governments of man have drifted into this. Behold, when a government no longer fills the needs of its people, God withdraws His heavenly protection from that government and the people run into anarchy.

Blame not the people for anarchy, assassinations and revolutions. The government is to blame in all cases. These conditions of vengeance are but the fruit resulting from the government's divergence from the will of Jehovah and the march of His light. Whenever a state sets up itself by violence against justice unto the multitude, the people fall upon that government and destroy it.

Finance, with its modern commercialism, corrupts all that it touches: the press, politics, education, and the church. Our competitive business system has so warped our moral judgement that not one man in a thousand realizes there is anything wrong in lobbying, bribery, and mis-representation. We are sold fruit jam made without fruit; butter that never saw a cow; all-wool goods that never came from an animal; medicines that kill instead of heal. Capitalism drains and brutalizes the workmen who do the work; haunts the business man with fear of failure, and makes him hard with success. It brutalizes our civilization, clogs the wheels of progress, and forever crowds us closer to the brink of destruction. When the three, church, state, and finance conspire against race and nation, all hell breaks loose.

Hitler's work is that of the great destroyer. His work is not finished. It has just begun. Before the next seven years have passed, when Hitler will have made his exit from the world stage, there will be a new Europe. Capitalism will have been destroyed; the present form of Christianity changed; a new League of Nations will have come and gone; and an epidemic of revolutions will have swept the governments of the "House of Have" into oblivion.

A classless society will be the result, but first the middle class will be liquidated and there will be but rich and poor. In the revolutions, the rich will be hunted down like rats. The horrors of the French Revolution will not only be repeated, but exceeded.

Impossible, you say? Have you forgotten what took

place in Russia? Are you unaware of the destruction of the landlords and land-owners in Poland when Stalin's troops marched in?

Is your heart filled with hate for all dictators? Do not hate, but pity them. The dictator who proclaims himself a god is taking upon himself the responsibilities and bondage of a god. It will take Hitler nine thousand years to undo the hell he is now creating. Rulership in this life means bondage in the after-life.

Centuries ago man was told, "He who lives by the sword shall die by the sword." Pity those with faith in the instruments of death rather than faith in the Voice of everlasting life.

The nations of the earth believe their power is in their armies and ships of war. In the next seven years they will be given such a diet of death as will make mankind allergic to armies and warfare for a thousand years to come.

Jesus taught the non-resistance of evil. The initiate knows well that evil is self-destroying. One often hears the remark, "How can God allow such things?" And generally the one making such a comment advocates the use of the law or other forceful means to annihilate the evil under discussion.

The Nazarene knew better. Those who live by the sword will die by the sword. Those spewing out hate will end in being hated, and those using force will arouse a greater force. The people of the United States need not worry about the conquest of our country by Hitler or any other warlord. Such men will be taken care of by the causes they themselves set into motion. Hitler's destruction of liberty of action and expression, both in his own country and conquered countries, will give birth to a revolution that will destroy him and his party.

Christian peoples have prayed for such a man as Hitler, although they had no idea that their prayers could only be answered by such a man of evil. For centuries, among all Christian peoples, a daily prayer has been, "Thy kingdom come, Thy will be done, on earth as it is in heaven."

What is God's kingdom? Is it capitalism, with its rich few at the top and its poverty-stricken millions at the bottom? Is it a chaos of religions and creeds? Is it a battle royal of nations? NO! If it is anything, it is a classless society with plenty for all. It must be based upon a faith wherein there can be no infidels, no atheists, no Jews, no gentiles, but a brotherhood of man acknowledging one father only, the All Highest. It can not be a world of clashing nationalisms, but one made up of a United States of the World.

For such a heaven upon earth to come into being, the following are requisite:

1. The four dominant world religions, with all their offspring of antagonistic creeds and dogmas, must be destroyed in order to make way for a new and better world religion.
2. All false race pride and egoistic nationalism must die before the fatherhood of God, the motherhood of the earth and the brotherhood of man can become an admitted fact. All artificial man-made barriers must be abolished, such as emigration laws, tariffs, custom duties, national armies, and other mediums of force wherewith capitalistic countries uphold their senile systems.
3. A new system of exchange must come into being. The international banking system, which finds its power in man-ordained gold, must be destroyed in order to make way for a new system of exchange based upon the fruit of the earth.

Hitler will conquer Europe, will destroy all national boundaries, and will incorporate present European peoples into a new confederacy of the nations, wherein there will be no customs or barriers. He is destroying the power of the bankers, and will sponsor a new medium of exchange not based upon gold.

It is not denied that Adolf Hitler is the embodiment of evil. We affirm that he is an ambassador of hell, a priest of chaos, head man of uz, creator of death. He is number 66, the number of war, nitrogen and death, a fit companion to number 666, which is the Pope. Great dark spiritual forces find their focus in Hitler, and he will destroy all lesser forces obstructing the march of the new day. He is the essence of evil, for he will eliminate many lesser evils. Hitler is the man foretold in so many prophecies as the one who would march with his legions during the Time of Trouble.

Adolf Hitler and his Fascist companions will fulfill the three pre-requisites mentioned above to the manifestation of the answer to the Lord's prayer.

1. Mussolini has declared himself to be the "Protector of Islam." Hitler is replacing within the Reich the religion of Christ with the religion of Hitler. His fifth columns in India are serving to sicken the peoples of the East with their Oriental religions. The same disintegration evident in Christianity is apparent in all Eastern religions. Soon the people will spew them all out.

2. Hitler is destroying national boundaries throughout Europe, and will soon form a confederacy of nations.

3. The war in Europe is not for the salvation of democracy or the destruction of Hitlerism. It is to determine who is to dominate Europe, England and the international bankers, or Hitler and the Third Reich. Hitler will soon sponsor a new medium of exchange with the mark of the false swastika on it, as foretold in the Bible. Hitler will destroy capitalism.

61

As evil is self-destructive, it is evident that Hitler has already brought into operation forces that will in turn destroy him within the next three and a half years. But the good that Hitler has accomplished will live after him. Following the time of destruction will come a time of reconstruction. Then—and not until then, will Christian prayers be answered.

CHAPTER V

PROPHECIES OF ASIA AND AFRICA

PROPHECIES OF INDIA

The seers of India have foretold a time when India would flow with blood. The following prophecy is taken from a book entitled, "Beasts, Men and Gods," by Ossendowski. The prophecy was given in 1890 to the Hutuku of the Narabanchi Monastery in Mongolia by an adept who is famous throughout India. The prediction pertains to the years 1914–1948.

"More and more people will forget their souls and will care about their bodies. . . . Great sin and corruption will reign upon earth. . . . The crowns of kings, great and small, will fall. . . . There will be a terrific world war. The seas will become red . . . the earth and the bottom of the seas will be strewn with bones . . . kingdoms will be scattered . . . whole peoples will die . . . hunger, disease, crimes unknown to law, never before seen in the world . . . the ancient roads will be covered with crowds wandering from place to place. . . . All the earth will be emptied. God will turn away from it and there will be only night and death. Then shall I send a people, now unknown, which shall tear out the weeds of madness and vice, and I will lead those who remain faithful to the spirit of man, in the fight against evil. They will found a new life upon earth purified by the death of nations. The most evil among mankind have not yet been born."

Paul Brunton, in his "Search in Secret India," mentions other prophecies foretelling the time when the British will be driven out of India and the country will become independent.

From observations of present political events in India, it seems that England will soon be forced to grant the demands of Gandhi and his party, and give complete independence to India.

JAPANESE PROPHECY

Japan has a prophecy dating back to 1793 which states:

When men fly like birds, ten great kings will go to war and the world will be under arms.

A picture of world conquest was painted for the Japanese people in 1926 by Prime Minister Tanaka in his Tanaka Memorial:

In order to conquer the world we must first conquer China. To conquer China we must first conquer Manchuria and Mongolia. Then all other countries of Asia will fear us and capitulate before us. The world will then understand that Eastern Asia is ours.

Although the authenticity of the Tanaka Memorial has been denied by Japan, the fact remains that every military move has been according to the plan of Tanaka. Regardless of any denials that Japan may make, the conquest of the United States is a part of Tanaka's plan of world conquest.

Following her defeat of Russia in 1905, a victory which led to her establishment as a military power, Japan began her imperialistic conquests of Korea, Manchuria and China. The aggressions of Japan in Asia are as much a part of the War of Armageddon, spoken of in the many prophecies pertaining to our times, as are the wars in Europe.

This War of Armageddon covers a 33-year cycle beginning with 1914 and lasting until 1948. Although there was an armistice in the European sector from 1918 to 1939, it affected a few nations only. Throughout the rest of the world, war has been continuous, accompanied in many places by revolution. Before this 33-year cycle is over, all nations will become involved.

The Japanese Islands will be destroyed in the coming continental changes. Japan has sown death in China. She will reap death in catastrophies of nature that will visit her island.

Russia—the Prophecy of Madam Blavatski

Madam Blavatski was one of the world's strangest women. She was a prolific writer, and the theosophical societies throughout the world are founded upon her work. Her name is well known to all students of occult and arcane subjects, and these students credit her with being one of the great prophets of the nineteenth century.

One of her most interesting prophecies follows:

When England ceases to carry the torch of democracy, out of Russia will come the greatest civilization the world has ever known.

England ceased to be a democracy within a few days after her declaration of war against Germany in 1939. England is now a dictatorship, and freedom is becoming as rare in the British Empire as it is in the Fascist and Nazi realms.

England has never been a *true* democracy, but has always been an autocracy of wealth. Now, like Germany, Italy, France and the U. S. S. R., she is a dictatorship.

In 1912, just before the World War, there appeared in "The Natal Advertiser" of Durban, Natal, South Africa, "a solemn warning that annihilation would come from all sources."

This warning was uttered by Margaret Scott Marshall, lecturer and seeress, and recorded by her husband, James Marshall. Two years later, Mrs. Marshall and her husband wrote their prophetic book entitled: *"1960: A Retrospect,"* which was ready for publication in 1916, but delayed until their coming to California, U. S. A. where the book was privately printed in 1919. It was written during the war, 1914–1918, and published in what the "Foreword" calls a "Lull in the Wars."

A respite given to the people to meditate on the past and prepare our minds to decide what course we shall pursue when the time of trial and testing comes again, as assuredly it will in the near future. . . . We have had some of the coming annihilation already, but it is a mere drop compared with what is to follow.

This book is couched in semi-story form and purports to be an account in detail of the present war of nations by some of the survivors of the terrible holocaust, and of the changed and beneficent conditions of human life following.

To quote a few pertinent sentences (looking backward a decade):

Although there had never been such a time of destruction, on the other hand there had never been such a revival . . . an awakening of men who were washed in the light of everlasting love.

The true heroes of that period of catastrophe were those who had, by reason of the divine principle within them, stood out from this welter of destruction and refused to be drawn into the dreadful maelstrom. . . . They recognized it to be a war of extermination . . . and operated in the mental world—which is the real world, the world of Cause—by concentrating strongly for peace, and throwing out the thought strongly into the universe, particularly at night time when the minds of men are receptive to such impressions.

The Master Mind assures us that had it not been for such minds working, consciously or unconsciously for peace, nothing could have saved our world from total annihilation.

These men, the Master Mind has declared, were the true leaders of the people, whilst He stigmatizes as traitors to mankind those who rushed their fellow-beings on the rocks of destruction.

The co-authors of *"1960: A Retrospect,"* are now living in Santa Barbara, California, and say, "We speak and write from the viewpoint of the interior world, not from the exterior, and appeal to the "God within." The same source is available for further teachings and prophecies."

CHAPTER VI

AMERICAN PROPHETS AND PROPHECIES

ANDREW JACKSON DAVIS

In Orange County, New York, in the year 1826, was born one of America's greatest prophets. Andrew Jackson Davis was able to cognize the world of spirit as clearly as the world of matter. During his lifetime he wrote many books that are spiritualistic classics. He was not only clairaudient and clairvoyant, he was also a great trance medium, and in 1845 at New York gave a series of lectures that attracted many of the leading minds of the country. Not only did he make predictions dealing with the general advancement of science and the development of our present age of machines, but he specifically described the Diesel-driven, streamlined trains that came into use about 1935.

> Instead of the present gallery-looking cars, there will be spacious saloons, almost portable dwellings, moving with such speed that there will be advertisements reading—"Through to California in four days."

He foretold the automobile, and stated that the time would come when they would be so constructed that no accident or collision would damage either passengers or baggage. Not only did he foresee our streamlined trains, but he also must have envisioned our trailer homes, for he said:

68

Look out about those days for carriages and traveling saloons on country roads—sans horses, sans steam, sans any visible motive power, moving with greater speed and safety than at present. Carriages will be moved by a simple mixture of aqueous and atmospheric gases—so easily condensed, so easily ignited, and so imparted by a machine somewhat resembling our engines, as to be entirely concealed between the forward wheels. The first requisite for these land locomotives will be good roads, upon which, with your engine, without your horses, you may travel with great rapidity.

Not only did he predict the automobile and stream-lined trains, but the airplane as well:

This power will not only move the locomotive on its rail and the carriage on the country road, but aerial cars also, which will move through the sky from country to country; and their beautiful influence will produce a universal brotherhood of acquaintance.

A. J. Davis foresaw the passing of the twelve and ten-hour day and the birth of a time when leisure will become the common lot. He foretold the invention of concrete, portable houses, the radio, and many more of our present commodities. Davis looked over and beyond the time of revolution and trouble in the United States to that time of peace and plenty pictured by Bellamy and other American prophets.

MORMON PROPHETS

The Mormon People, adherents of the Church of Jesus Christ of Latter-day Saints, with headquarters in Salt Lake City, Utah, hold to the belief that prophecy is as common today as in ancient times. Many of the prophecies given by their founder and first prophet, Joseph Smith, have been fulfilled. One of Smith's most interesting prophecies, given in 1843, is entitled the "White Horse Prophecy."

You will go to the Rocky Mountains and will establish a great and mighty people which I call the White Horse of Peace and Safety. You will see the constitution of the United States almost destroyed; it will hang by a thread as fine as the finest silk fiber. I love the Constitution; it was made under the inspiration of God, and will be preserved and saved by the efforts of the White Horse and the Red Horse who will come to its defense. A terrible revolution will take place in America such as has never been before, for the land will be literally left without a supreme government, and every species of wickedness will be rampant. It will be so terrible that father will be against son, mother against daughter and daughter against mother. The most terrible scenes of murder, bloodshed and rapine that has ever been looked on will take place. Peace will be taken from the earth. The Turkist Empire of the Crescent will be the first great power to be disrupted.* England and France will be allied together in order to keep Russia from conquering the world. While the terrible revolution is going on England and France will try to make peace in the United States. They will find the United States so broken up, many claiming authority, still there will be no responsible government. Then it will appear to other countries that England has taken possession of the country. The Black Horse (India) will join Russia. Armed with British bayonets, the doings of the Black Horse will be terrible. There is a land in the Rocky Mountains that will be invaded by the Japanese unless care is taken. The last struggle that Zion (America) will face will be when the whole of America is made the Zion of our God.

Brigham Young, after the death of Joseph Smith at Carthage, Illinois, in 1844, led the Mormons in their great migration to Utah, for it had been prophesied to them that Utah was the safest place on the continent during the great earthquakes and continental changes to come. Mormon prophesies state that changes foretold would take place within the next hundred years or by 1944. Evidently Joseph Smith's vision extended for a century, for a civil war has been predicted by many for

* Joseph Smith erred in stating that Turkey would be the first government to be disrupted. The Russian Empire was overthrown in 1917, the Ottoman Empire in 1923.

the years 1941–45 in the United States of America.

Orson Pratt, another of the early Mormon prophets, also mentions a second civil war in the Journal of Discourses, Vol. 20:

What then will be the condition of the people when the great and dreadful war will come? It will be very different from the war between the North and South. It will be neighborhood against neighborhood, city against city, town against town, state against state, and they will go forth destroying and being destroyed. Manufacturing will almost cease, great cities will be left desolate. The time will come when the great city of New York will be left without inhabitants.

Another prophecy published in Mormon literature in March 1922 gives another preview of the coming chaos. This prevision was given to a non-Mormon but told to a Mormon:

I saw first a brief sketch of the present state of the world. Each country in turn was shown, and in my mind was formed, from some source, the words, "as it is today."

I then saw a new international war break out with its center upon the Pacific Ocean, but sweeping and encircling the globe. I saw the opposing forces were roughly divided by so-called Christianity on one side, and so-called followers of Mohammed and Buddha on the other side. I saw a world-wide dislocation and devastation of production and slaughter of people occur more swiftly and upon a larger scale than ever before. I saw those of a faith similar to yours in the Far East begin to look to Palestine for safety.

I saw the international war automatically break down, and national revolutions occur in every country and complete the work of chaos and desolation. I saw geological disturbances occur which helped in this work as if it were intended to do so.

I saw the international boundry line disappear as these two governments (Canada and the U. S.) broke up and dissolved in chaos. I saw race rioting upon this American continent on a vast scale.

I saw hunger and starvation in this world, a granary of the American continent swept off in vast numbers of these conflicting elements. I saw disease produced by hunger, strife and chaos, complete the end of the present order. My impression was that from the outbreak of the international war, these things developed in a continuous procession and almost ran concurrently, as it is with sickness, the various symptoms are all in evidence at one and the same time, but in different stages of development.

Another Mormon prophecy is that of Brigham Young, and is found in his "Discourses," pages 170–172:

All that you now know can scarcely be called a preface to the sermon that will be preached with fire and sword, tempests, earthquakes, hail, rain and fearful destruction. What matter the destruction of a few railway cars? You will hear of magnificent cities now idolized by the people sinking in the earth entombing the inhabitants. The sea will heave itself beyond its bounds engulfing many cities. Famine will spread over the nations, and nation will rise against nation, kingdom against kingdom, states against states, in our own country and in foreign lands.

Marie Ogden and the "Home of Truth"

The Mormon prophecies are concurred in by hundreds of prophecies of similar vein coming through mediums all over the world. The writer is not interested in such prophecies unless he has complete confidence in the sincerity and integrity of the source.

Ten years ago a plan for the formation of a place of refuge during the coming years was given to Marie M. Ogden, a psychic sensitive in whose sincerity there can be no question. The information coming through this sensitive is in accord with Mormon prophecies, although Mrs. Ogden is not a Mormon.

In 1933 Marie Ogden, with a small group of believers in her inspiration, founded a colony between

Moab and Monticello, Utah, on Highway 450, which is known as Home of Truth. The founders put everything they owned into the colony, and have since worked unceasingly to promote the various departments of the community. Members have, on occasion, worked for outsiders and used their wages to purchase livestock and building materials.

No record has been kept of the many persons who have stopped at the colony for aid, food, shelter, and many times for wearing apparel. Many left without notice, took what was given without thanks, and some even came back and stole what they wanted. The early days of the colony were hard indeed, but with 1938 the tide changed, and from that date both material and spiritual progress has been rapid.

As early as January, 1938, information came about the disruption of our present money system, prophesying that the needy will become so disheartened that they will take the law into their own hands and demand food and the necessities of life.

Excerpts from the inspired writings of Marie Ogden follow:

The wranglings and the bitterness in the hearts of men will increase, and soon the mighty conflict will get into full swing. The oppressed will rise up against those who hold the power, and so will the overthrow of a nation begin.

The mighty ones will have cause to quake with fear, although they will fight desperately to maintain their position, and the right to control the masses.

While this is in progress, Nature will be at work in other quarters to add to the fury and turmoil, and another form of destruction will get under way. Great and terrible will be the havoc wrought in certain quarters. As in the days of Noah, the greater numbers will go their merry way unmindful of the times until they, too, shall be caught in the vortex, and only then will they realize that a just God is meting out punishment for the evil wrought. It will be like unto nothing ever experienced in your land of beauty and abundance of God's wealth. Those who are among the downtrodden will strive to take the law in their own hands. Only as the hatred and fury of a downtrodden people breaks those who sit in high places and hold the power and riches of the land, will they be made to realize that their power is as nothing; although equally violent acts against their accusers will be used to control the situation.

Riot will break loose, and after the storm of battle subsides there will come a brief lull, during which a new form will be set up as a means of compromise. This, however, will be but temporary, since the destruction to be wrought will be incomplete, and the new form will be but a gesture to quell the feeling of hatred among the people.

This is the picture as we view it from these realms, and because there must needs be a time of strife before the end, there is rejoicing in the heavens that the time of action is approaching. Only through adversity can the adjustments of the future come into fulfillment. . . . So will all things work together for good and so will the mighty upheaval get into full swing to offset the injustices of the past, for it is not intended that the wealth and the abundance of your earth be in the hands of a few, nor is it intended that men make laws which protect only the rich and powerful ones.

In February of 1938, she was again warned of the need to prepare for darker days ahead:

Great and ominous clouds are gathering over the countries where the war-lords count not the dangers to the peoples over whom they rule, nor do they care what becomes of the rank and file who compose the masses. So great is their ambition for power in the sight of man that they see not beyond the confines of their mortal minds. . . . So steeped in selfishness are they that they seem as the tyrants of ancient days who demanded of their subjects to obey their word of command. . . . These are the things to think on as you consider the misery in the world among the oppressed and the depressed who are as pawns on a chess board for their leaders.

In March of 1939 came more information in regard to Nature's disruption and more about the economic breakdown, from which we quote in part:

The rugged Pacific coast, which I saw destroyed in vision, will be resolved into a less hazardous place as the waters recede gradually, and will permit man's descent to reclaim what may be salvaged of the ruins. The new land rising out in the Pacific ocean will be explored only when a new generation has been raised and as later inventions of man permit such venture.

In the interim much will transpire within the territory you occupy (Utah) which will be as the center of attraction for the coming generation of mankind since the eastern part of the un-United States shall undergo such disruption and change as to make of it a place of similar desolation for a long period of time; and henceforth shall it be an unfit place of habitation except in the selected and chosen territory of the original use (the Thirteen Colonies) when the white man first set foot thereon.

Water shall abound everywhere beyond the mountainous region to the east of you, and shall surround the remaining surface of the earth, where land to be repopulated and reclaimed at a later date will remain, and when the purification thereof is completed.

Before these greater changes can come into being, a great purging of the souls of men must get under way in order that the purification to be wrought may be complete; and when only those who are of willing heart to serve in the New Age may gather together in safe places when these greater changes come. . . .

Early in April 1939, came another bit of information concerning the "Time of Tribulation":

The "time of the end" of the age of materialism and greed is fast approaching, wherein mankind must "look to God" and renew his contact with the Divine Source in order to carry on in the New Age.

The rise and fall of man is a sign that God is taking account of the works of mankind, and when the mighty power to be let loose over the earth shall hold sway everything that is of God shall remain intact, and everything that is of Mammon shall be levelled to the ground. . . .

Know further that these things shall come to pass *within the next decade* in order that the iniquity of past ages may be resolved into nothingness, and the new order of living be established in all fullness thereof. . . . The blending of the two shall mark the end of the reign of man as a law unto himself, and only as those who think not beyond their own interests and desires are made to see the folly of their ways through the utter breakdown of their system and methods of living, shall they become aware of their foolishness.

By the same token shall they become aware that those who put their trust in God, and those who look not to man, or to man-made laws, but take counsel with God *are* making headway. So shall the judgment be meted out in no uncertain way, and while it shall cause unrest to those who are to be given their last chance to reform their ways, and greater fear to those who think only on themselves, it shall likewise cause happiness to those who have lived in harmony with Higher Law, which is so little understood by the average person in life today.

Few there are who give much thought to their inner nature, as they seek means of livelihood in a world ruled by those who hold the power for the moment, and to whom they must look for sustenance.

But, dear friends, keep ever in mind that "out of evil cometh good" and when the smoke of battle is cleared away, and when the old order is wiped out, there shall come glorious opportunity to set up the new kingdom and the brotherhood of man. Then shall the further progress of man continue in a finer and bigger way than ever before, because then what man desires for himself he shall also want for his fellow man. So shall we come into the time of the "1000 years of peace to reign on earth" and the Sabbath day of rest wherein man may enjoy the fruits of his labor in a more bountiful way. Such is the picture as we view it, and toward which goal we are working.

The vision presented to this remarkable woman, and the information given the world through her, pertaining to a change in the axis of the earth, the rising of the lost continent of Pan or Mu in the Pacific, and the inundation of parts of various countries in both hemispheres, is in harmony with prophecies received during the nineteenth century by the Essenes and now on file in their archives.

A prophecy in the Essene archives is similar to the Mormon and the Ogden prophecies. This augury was written by John Ballou Newbrough in July, 1889, over a half century ago:

According to the latest calculations, we have fifty-eight years yet ahead to get ready in (1889 plus 58 years brings us to the year 1947). At or before that time all the present governments, religious and all moneyed monopolies are to be overthrown and go out of existence. This prophecy is figured by mathematical rules and figures.

The increase in unrest in society is an unmistakable sign foreshadowing what is to come to the great masses of people in a short time.

Various combinations of capital and labor are signs of increasing weakness. Extremes so opposite must culminate in destruction. Mathematically, it seems just as certain as a collision when two trains are approaching on the same track. To prevent the coming calamity, many combinations will be resorted to. Our present form of so-called Christian religion will overrun America, tear down the American flag and trample it underfoot. In Europe the disaster will be even more terrible. Capital will back up the church in persecution, general anarchy will follow and hundreds of thousands of people will be killed. In China and India so terrible will be the fall that words cannot describe it. All nations will be demolished and all the earth be thrown open to all people to go and come as they please.

There is much evidence indicating that the so-called Christian religion will soon overrun America, tear down the American flag, and trample it under foot. Fascism, camouflaging under the terms "Americanism" and "Christianity," will rule the United States within three years. There are today more than 800 organizations active in bringing Fascism to the United States. In the forefront of this drive is an alien Catholic priest, Charles E. Coughlin, and his National Union for Social Justice.

Father Coughlin can be held directly responsible for the inspiration leading to the organization of the following listed racial-hatred groups:

Christian Worker's Alliance
Christian Vigilante Front—Brooklyn, strong arm group
Christian Index—Ebling's Casino
Christian Congress—speaker's group
Christian Minutemen—strong arm group
Christian Edifiers and Christian Pioneers
Christian Defenders
Christian Protective League
Christian Order of Coughlinites
American Brotherhood of Christian Congresses, radio stock sellers for
    Coughlin
Christian American League
Christian Defense League—composed of lawyers
Crusaders for Christian Social Justice
Christian Merchants and Consumers League
Social Justice Distributors Club
Christian Phalanx

Other organizations interested in the propagation of Fascism in America are:

Crusaders of Americanism, Inc.
American Patriots, Inc.
American Nationals
Anti-Communist Women's League
German-American Bund
A.B.C. Legion
Silver Legion of William Dudley Pelley
The White Camellias of George Deatherage
Crusaders or White Shirts of George W. Christians

A few individuals listed in the March 6th, 1939, issue of Life Magazine as active in the development of Fas-

78

cism, are: Gerald E. Winron of Wichita, Kansas; Robert E. Edmonson, publisher of American Vigilante Bulletins; James True, publisher of Washington "Dope Letter"; Edward W. Hunter of Boston, head of the anti-union Industrial Defense Association; Senator Robert Reynolds of North Carolina; and Major George Van Horn Moseley.

The claim that Henry Ford is the financial angel back of Coughlin seems confirmed by the frequent conferences of Harry Bennett, Ford Motor Company's publicity man, with Father Coughlin and Major Moseley.

The shirt movement started some years ago by the Ku Klux Klan in America, afterward spread to Italy, with its Black Shirts, and to Germany, with its Brown Shirts. In recent years it bounced back to the U. S. A., brought the Silver, White, and other shirts of varied hues, spread back across the seas to England, where Sir Oswald Moseley started his Black Shirts, then to Brazil, influencing Plinio Salgado to start his Green Shirts, and into the Irish Free State, which gave birth to General Erin O'Duffy and his Blue Shirts. Joseph, with his coat of many colors, was a piker, it seems.

> "Pelley, with his Silver Shirts, his back against the wall,
> Hitler, with his Brown Shirts, lording over all,
> Mussolini's Black Shirts, riding for a fall,
> Three cheers for Mahatma Gandhi, with no shirt at all."

THE MARCH OF FASCISM IN THE U. S. A.

Fascism will hide under the cloak of Christianity, and will conceal its gangsterism behind a shield labeled

FREEDOM, DEMOCRACY, and AMERICANISM.

The country has not been without its warnings of the trouble ahead. Here are three prophecies that have been printed many times, but are well worth your attention. The following story of Washington's vision rests upon the veracity of two men, Anthony Sherman and Wesley Bradshaw. Anthony Sherman, to whom was told the vision by Washington, was a soldier in the Revolutionary Army, and his name is to be found on army records. Sherman was about eighteen years old at the time he was told of the vision, and he lived to be ninety-nine years old. The story was recorded by Wesley Bradshaw, to whom Anthony Sherman recounted it shortly before his death.

GENERAL WASHINGTON'S VISION

by

Wesley Bradshaw

Originally Published in The National Tribune,
Vol. 4, No. 12. Dec. 1880.

The last time I ever saw Anthony Sherman was on the Fourth of July, 1859, in Independence Square. He was then ninety-nine years old, and becoming feeble. But though so old, his dimming eyes rekindled as he gazed upon Independence Hall, which he came to visit once more.

"Let us go into the hall," he said. "I want to tell you an incident of Washington's life—one which no one alive knows of except myself; and, if you live, you will, before long, see it verified.

"From the opening of the Revolution we experienced all phases of fortune, now good and now ill, one time victorious and another conquered. The darkest period we had, I think, was when Washington, after several reverses, retreated to Valley Forge, where he resolved to pass the winter of 1777. Ah. I have often seen the tears coursing down our dear commander's careworn cheeks, as he would be conversing with confidential officers about the condition of his poor soldiers. You have doubtless heard the story of Washington's going to the thicket to pray. Well, it was not only true, but he used often to pray in secret for aid and comfort from God, the interposition of whose Divine Providence brought us safely through the darkest days of tribulation.

"One day—I remember it well, the chilly wind whistling through the leafless trees, though the sky was cloudless and the sun shone brightly—he remained in his quarters nearly all afternoon alone.

"When he came out I noticed that his face was a shade paler than usual, and there seemed to be something on his mind of more than ordinary importance. Returning just after dusk, he dispatched an orderly to the quarters of an officer, who was presently in attendance. After a preliminary conversation of about half an hour Washington, gazing upon his companion with that strange look of dignity which he alone could command, said:

"I do not know whether it is owing to the anxiety of my mind or what, but this afternoon, as I was sitting at this table engaged in preparing a dispatch, something seemed to disturb me. Looking up, I beheld standing opposite a singularly beautiful female. So astonished was I, for I had given strict orders not to be disturbed, that it was some moments before I found language to inquire the purpose of her presence. A second, a third, and even a fourth time did I repeat my question, but received no answer from my mysterious visitor, except a slight raising of her eyes. By this time I felt strange sensations spreading through me. I would have risen, but the riveted gaze of the being before me rendered volition impossible. I assayed once more to address her, but my tongue had become useless. Even thought itself had become paralyzed. A new influence, mysterious, potent, irresistible, took possession of me. All I could do was to gaze steadily, vacantly at my unknown visitant. Gradually the surrounding atmosphere seemed filled with sensations, and grew luminous. Everything about me seemed to rarefy; the mysterious visitor herself becoming more airy and yet more distinct to my sight than before. I now began to feel as one dying, or rather to experience the sensation which I have sometimes imagined accompanies dissolution. I did not think, I did not reason, I did not move. All, alike, were impossible. I was conscious only of gazing fixedly, vacantly, at my companion.

"Presently I heard a voice saying, 'Son of the Republic, look and learn'; while at the same time my visitor extended her arm eastwardly. I now beheld a heavy white vapor at some distance rising fold upon fold. This gradually dissipated, and I looked upon a strange scene. Before me lay spread out in one vast plain all the countries of the world—Europe, Asia, Africa, and America. I saw rolling and tossing between Europe and America, the billows of the Atlantic; and between Asia and America lay the Pacific. 'Son of the Republic,' said the mysterious voice as before, 'look and learn.'

"At that moment I beheld a dark, shadowy being, like an angel, standing, or rather floating, in mid-air between Europe and America. Dipping water out of the ocean in the hollow of each hand, he sprinkled some upon America with his right hand, while with his left hand he cast some on Europe. Immediately a cloud arose from these countries, and joined in mid-ocean. For a while it remained stationary, and then it moved slowly westward, until it enveloped America in its murky folds. Sharp flashes of lightning gleamed through it at intervals; and I heard the smothered groans and cries of the American people. A second time the angel dipped water from the ocean and sprinkled it out as before. The dark cloud was then drawn back to the ocean, in whose heaving billows it sank from view. A third time I heard the mysterious voice saying, 'Son of the Republic, look and learn.' I cast my eyes upon America and beheld villages and towns and cities springing up one after another until the whole land, from the Atlantic to the Pacific, was dotted with them. Again I heard the mysterious voice say, 'Son of the Republic, the end of the century cometh. Look and learn.'

"And with this, the dark, shadowy figure turned its face southward, and from Africa I saw an ill-omened spectre approach our land. It flitted slowly over every town and city of the latter. The inhabitants presently set themselves in battle array against each other. As I continued looking I saw a bright angel on whose brow rested a crown of light on which was traced the word 'Union,' place an American flag between the divided nation, and say, 'Remember, ye are brethren.' Instantly, the inhabitants, casting from them their weapons, became friends once more, and united around the National Standard.

"And again I heard the mysterious voice saying, 'Son of the Republic, look and learn.' At this, the dark, shadowy angel placed a trumpet to his mouth and blew three distinct blasts; and taking water from the ocean, he sprinkled it upon Europe, Asia, and Africa. Then my eyes beheld a fearful scene: from each of these countries arose thick, black clouds that were soon joined into one. And throughout this mass there gleamed a dark-red light, by which I saw hordes of armed men, who, moving with the cloud, marched by land and sailed by sea to America; which country was enveloped in the volume of cloud. And I dimly saw these vast armies devastate the whole country and burn the villages, towns, and cities that I beheld springing up.

"As my ears listened to the thundering of the cannon, the clashing of swords, and the shouts and cries of millions in mortal combat, I again heard the mysterious voice saying, 'Son of the Republic look and learn.' As the voice ceased, the shadowy angel, for the last time, dipped water from the ocean and sprinkled it upon America. Instantly the dark cloud rolled back, together with the armies it had brought, leaving the inhabitants of the land victorious.

"Then once more I beheld the villages, towns, and cities springing up where I had seen them before; while the bright angel, planting the azure standard he had brought in the midst of them, cried in a loud voice: 'While the stars remain and the heavens send down dew upon the earth, so long shall the Union last.' And taking from his brow the crown on which was blazoned the word 'Union,' he placed it upon the Standard, while people, kneeling down, said, 'Amen!'

"The scene instantly began to fade and dissolve, and I at last saw nothing but the rising, curling vapor I at first beheld. This also disappearing, I found myself once more gazing upon the mysterious visitor who, in the same voice I had heard before, said, 'Son of the Republic, what you have seen is thus interpreted. Three great perils will come upon the Republic. The most fearful for her is the third: but the whole world united shall not prevail against her. Let every child of the Republic learn to live for his God, his land, and his Union.' With those words the vision vanished, and I started from my seat and felt that I had seen a vision; wherein had been shown me the birth, progress, and destiny of the United States."

"Such, my friend," concluded the venerable narrator, "were the words I heard from Washington's own lips; and America will do well to profit by them."

The following prophecy was found in the journal of Joseph Hoag, who was a Quaker, or member of the Society of Friends. His grandson, Thomas Hoag, lived at Waubeek, Iowa, in 1896, and had the journal in which the vision was recorded. Joseph Hoag was born in 1762, and at the time of the vision was forty-one years old.

"In the year of 1803, probably in the eighth or ninth month, I was one day alone in the fields, and observed that the sun shone clear, but that a mist eclipsed the brightness of its shining. As I reflected upon the singularity of the event, my mind was struck into a silence, the most solemn I ever remembered to have witnessed, for it seemed that all my faculties were laid low and brought into an unusually deep silence. And I said to myself, 'What can this mean? I do not recollect ever before to have been sensible to such feelings.' And I heard a voice from Heaven say, 'This that thou seest which dims the brightness of the sun, is a sign of the coming times. I took the forefathers of the Country from a land of oppression; I planted them here among people of the forest; I sustained them; and while they were humble, I blessed them; and fed them and they have become a numerous people. But they have now become too proud and lifted up, and have forgotten Me who nourished and protected them in the wilderness, and they are running into every abomination and evil practice of which the old countries are guilty and I have suffered a dividing spirit to come among them. Lift up thine eyes and behold.'

"And I saw them dividing in great heat. This division began in the church upon points of doctrine. It went through various religious denominations, and in its progress and its course, the effect was nearly the same. Those who dissented went off with high heads and taunting language; and those who kept to their organized sentiments, appeared excited and sorrowful; and when this dividing spirit entered the society of Friends, it raged in as high degree there as any I had before discovered. As before, those who separated went off with haughty looks and taunting, censuring language. Those who kept to their ancient principles retired by themselves.

"It next appeared in the lodges of the Free Masons, and it broke out in appearance like a volcano, inasmuch as it set the country in an uproar for a length of time. Then it entered politics throughout the United States and did not stop until it produced a cavil war, and an abundance of human blood was shed in the course of the combat. The Southern States lost their power, and slavery was abolished from their borders.

"THEN A MONARCHIAL POWER AROSE—TOOK THE GOVERNMENT OF THE STATES—ESTABLISHED A NATIONAL RELIGION AND MADE ALL SOCIETIES TRIBUTARY TO THE SUPPORT OF ITS EXPENSES. I saw them take property from the Friends to a large amount and, amazed, I heard a voice proclaim: 'THIS POWER SHALL NOT ALWAYS STAND: BUT WITH THIS POWER I WILL CHASTISE MY CHURCH UNTIL THEY RETURN TO THE FAITHFULNESS OF THEIR FOREFATHERS. Thou seest what is coming on thy native land for their iniquity and the blood of Africa, the remembrance of which has come up before Me. This vision is yet for many days.' "

I had no idea of writing it down for many years, until it became such a burden that for my own relief I have written it.

(signed) Joseph Hoag.

THE VISION OF GENERAL McCLELLAND

General McClelland, at two o'clock of the third night after his arrival in Washington to take command of the Union Army, was working on his maps. In relating the experience, the General stated that he passed into a trance-like condition during which he heard a voice and was given a vision of the placement of enemy troops that enabled him to prevent a Confederate victory. The only part of the vision of interest now is that which pertains to the future. Here is McClelland's story:

For a while previous to this, however, I had been conscious of a shining light on my left that steadily increased until the moment I ceased my task, when it became, in an instant, more intense than the noonday sun. Quickly I raised my eyes, and never, were I to live forever, should I forget what I saw. The dim, shadowy figure was no longer a dim, shadowy one, but a glorified refulgent figure of Washington, Father of His Country, and now, for a second time, its savior.

My friend, it would be utterly impossible for me to attempt to describe the majesty of that returned spirit. I can only say that Washington, as I beheld him in my dream (or trance as you may choose to call it), was the most God-like being I could have ever conceived of. Like a weak, dazzled bird, I sat gazing at the heavenly vision from the sweet and silent repose of Mount Vernon. Our Washington had risen, to once more encircle and raise up with his saving arm our fallen and bleeding country. As I continued looking, an expression of sublime benignity came gently upon his visage, and for the last time I heard that slow, solemn voice saying something like this:

"General McClelland, while yet in the flesh I beheld the birth of the American Republic. It was indeed a hard and bloody one, but God's blessing was upon the nation, and therefore, through this great struggle for existence, He sustained her with His mighty hand and brought her out triumphantly. A century has not passed since then, and yet the child republic has taken her position, a peer with nations whose pages of history extend for ages into the past. She has (since those dark days, by the favor of God) greatly prospered, and now, by the very reason of this prosperity, she has been brought to her second great struggle, this, so far the most perilous ordeal she has to endure, is to pass, as she is, from childhood to opening maturity.

"She is called on to accomplish that vast result—self-conquest; to learn that important lesson—self-control, self-rule, that in the future will place her in the van of power and civilization. It is here that all the nations have hitherto failed, and she, too—the republic of the earth, had not God willed otherwise—would by tomorrow's sunset, have been a heap of stones, cast up over the final grave of human liberty. But her cries have come up out of the borders like sweet incense unto heaven. She shall be saved. Then shall peace once more be upon her, and prosperity shall fill her with joy. But her mission will not then be finished, for ere another century shall have gone by, THE OPPRESSORS OF THE WHOLE EARTH, hating and envying her and her exaltation, SHALL JOIN THEMSELVES TOGETHER AND RAISE UP THEIR HANDS AGAINST

HER. But if she be found worthy of her high calling, they shall be truly discomfited and then will be ended her third and last struggle for existence. Henceforth, shall the Republic go on, increasing in goodness and power, until her borders shall end only in the remotest corners of the earth, and the whole earth shall, beneath her shadowy wings, become a universal republic.

"Let her in prosperity, however, remember the Lord her God.

"Let her trust in Him and she shall never be confounded."

The heavenly visitant ceased speaking, and as I still continued gazing on him, drew near to me and raised and placed his hands above. No sound now passed his lips, but I felt a strange influence coming over me. I inclined my head to receive his blessing, "the baptism of the spirit of Washington." The following instant peals of thunder rolled in upon me, and I awoke. The visitor had departed and I again was sitting in my apartment with everything exactly as it was before I fell asleep, with a few exceptions. The maps of which I had dreamed I had been marking were literally covered with a net of pencil signs and figures. I arose to my feet and rubbed my eyes, and took a turn or two around the room to recover myself. I was awake, but the pencilings were as plain as ever. I had before me as complete a map and repository of information as though I had spent several years in gathering and recording its details.

Another American prophecy is that found in a book written in California, purportedly while the author was under the control of an unseen master. This book, "A Dweller on Two Planets," was written in 1884. This prophecy is in agreement with many others and is being confirmed by the signs of the times.

During many, many centuries prophecy hath looked forward to the end of the Age as a time of awful woe, and has pictured dread scenes of terminal horror. Am I come to say that all these predictions shall fail? Is the Book of the Apocalypse mere allegory? Would it were! Shall America, the glorious, together with the rest of the world, meet similar woe? Alas, worse, though not by water, but by fire. Shall all be wiped out of existence leaving a planet in ruins? Unto the end of full obedience and the coming into harmony with divine law shall the lash be applied; words may not portray the scenes. This is the Message of the End of the Age:

The hour hath struck. And yet in all of this there is no mystery, no supernatural penalty, no capricious infliction by an offended personal God, and nothing of "man's necessity, God's opportunity." It is all of man's own doing. He hath wandered from the Way, and hath for the God-nature in him, which he should have revered and nourished, substituted worship of self and of mammon; hath cast out love, and placed violence, lust, greed and all the riotous animalism in him in command of his life. Man is his own judge and executioner. Man is the type and the universe is the print; nature patterns after man, not man after nature. He, a being of free-will, hath brought all coming woes of judgment to be inevitable; he must endure, as he hath sown; so must he reap. O Man! forgetter of love, of mercy, of right; breeder of hate, of cruelty, and of the inhumanity that hath and still doth make countless millions mourn, is it possible that thou hast been blind to the handwriting on the wall? Alas, yes, thou hast! Rampant is the spirit of selfishness, of greed, of merciless gain; its hand guides the trains and steamers, clicks the telegraph keys, operates the telephone and cables, makes a mockery of free speech, shackles the press so that it dares to utter only that which cannot offend its master; every human enterprise, all national policies and international committees, all things, even the churches, are willing vassals to this fiend, SELF. What then? Ruin is on all sides, the human race and all lower creatures its victims. Masons at work on a high wall shout as a brick falls: "Stand from under!"

Aye, stand from under! A world is falling! Frenzied millions of men and women, boys and girls, no longer free save in name, are menaced with starvation. Hungry, cold, half-clad, shelterless only too often, denied the chance to work, however willing they may be, corporation-owned machinery their competitor; monopoly and trust-ridden, sleeping or waking. This inhuman picture is the rule, not the exception. Thou knowest this full well. I state nothing new in this regard, and the awful facts are under-drawn instead of exaggerated. All of this, although in far, far less degree, has been so at the ending of every age. But it can never be so again after this for HERE THE WAY DIVIDES.

In the full time by fire the Reaper shall reap, and no place be found for physical safety by the unchanged heart. But the time of it shall be foreshortened, else no flesh could remain alive. Stand from under! The roar of armed hosts must succeed the thunderous mutterings of the times. No more is there any chance to prevent the coming retribution (albeit it may seem unduly deferred), for the causes have had their way. Too late is it even to modify the result of the misguidance of that spirit whose hand sways the helm. A short, but sharp conflict, sanguinary past belief, even now reddens on the horizon. The trained armies, millions of men active or in reserve, that are now engaged in conquest, fevered with war, will but little longer, comparatively, submit to having themselves and loved ones ground under the heel and strangled by the hand of that organized thing, capital, which, itself is merely the natural fruit of selfishness, none the less is a riotous animal principle, compelling the few to be masters of the many, denying the God-born declaration that all men are created free and equal, and warping it to seem a giant lie.

Soon millions of trained soldiers will turn upon the visible representatives, the wealthy and worldly prosperous, who in reality are not more responsible than will be their assailants, of that relentless force behind all human enterprise. Later they will break up into lawless bands, each self-server's hand weaponed against his fellow creatures. Then will the pent-up hate, the savagery and selfishness begotten by ages of selfishness ruled by unbridled animalism break in a storm such as the world hath never yet seen, no, not during all the ages I scan.

That loveless conflict will initiate that which, nature completing, will leave living but one where now are many. Hard and fast after the human conflict will come pestilences unparalleled, sweeping the wide earth over, for in that day none will pause to bury the slain until the evil is wrought, nor then, for the dead of the plagues will be as thousands for every one by violence. And all this because the love that should grace and soften men's hearts, each for all and all for each, dried up and became a mockery in the close of the ended cycle, leaving but scattered cases, few and far between.

Nature follows man. Wherefore the waters of the earth will dry out, rains be withheld, cyclones sweep, and an earthquake come such as was not since man was on the earth. But all of this will occur only through natural causes, and in consonance with the selfishness, lust, greed, anger and general depravity of the type. As these blaze in

89

the human breast, so shall the air, dry and vaporless under brazen skies, develop solar heats more fierce than history ever knew. A parched earth, furnace-like, piling all flesh mountain high; pestilences stalking unchecked. O ye! Blind to the handwriting on the wall, which flickers still, though writ for a spent cycle. Turn now and read while yet the last midnight stroke reverberates.

When will these things be? *When you see Jerusalem surrounded by encampments, you may know that desolation is near.*

The armies are beginning to gather around Jerusalem. Britain recently sent reinforcements into Palestine to put down clashes between Jews and Arabs, and to guard against a new wave of bloody terror sweeping the Holy Land.

Keep your eye on Palestine. Many prophecies point to the Holy Land as the barometer of the next few years.

PHILIP DRU: ADMINISTRATOR

THE PROPHECY OF COLONEL EDWARD MANDELL HOUSE

During the winter of 1911 Colonel House, who a few years later came into national power as adviser and alter ego of Woodrow Wilson, was ill at his home in Texas. During his convalescence he wrote the manuscript for a book published the following year titled "Philip Dru: Administrator." This book, now out of print, *is a remarkable prophecy*. A flexible currency based upon commercial assets, old age pensions, unemployment insurance, graduated income and excess profits taxes and several other progressive suggestions have become laws of the nation since the book was written. The most noteworthy prophecy awaits fulfillment. It foretells the American dictator:

90

Philip Dru was a West Point graduate who resigned from the army following injury to his eyes and went into social service work. A conspiracy of Wall Street to secure absolute control over the legislative and administrative branches of the government was discovered which led to a revolt of the people. Philip Dru assumed command of the insurgents, marched upon Washington, D. C., defeated the regulars, took over the government and became dictator. During the seven years of Philip Dru's term as administrator, he revised the laws, reformed the courts, rewrote the constitution, eliminated the rich owning and governing class, introduced an economy of abundance and returned the government to the people. A new Monroe Doctrine was formulated, the Americas unified, and harmony established between the U. S. A. and all other nations.

Considering that "Philip Dru: Administrator" was written by Colonel House long before the epidemic of dictators, totalitarian states, fascism and world wars, it is indeed a strange coincidence to find present events pointing to fulfillment of the prophecy of Colonel House foretelling the rise of a beneficient dictator. It appears, however, that we will first be cursed, between the years of 1941 and 1945, with a malign form of fascist dictatorship.

CHAPTER VII

Prophecies from the Spirit World

Prophecies from the Land of Spirit

The following opinions of the state of the nation and of the world were given shortly after the end of the war of 1914–1918.

Messages from the spirit world have been coming to our three dimensional world with increasing frequency since the beginning in 1848 of the cycle of Kosmon. As the views that follow are all those of men who occupied a prominent place in government during the years they lived on earth, we will find them worthy of our consideration.

Like attracts like upon every plane of existence. This is a rule operative throughout the universe. People go to an uneducated medium living in filth and squalor, and expect to receive messages from heaven. Common sense should tell them that clear water is not to be had from a muddy pool. If one expects messages of worth from our unseen helpers, is it not reasonable to assume that one must find a medium who is of like caliber in mind, morals and character to the one from whom light is sought?

The following messages purport to be from several of the men who were leading minds during the years in which they lived on earth. The medium through whom these messages came was also possessed of mind and talent on a plane with his unseen visitors. Francis Grierson was a poet, an outstanding musician, a leading writer on "The New Age" of London, a friend of the intelligensia, eminent in philosophy, art, music, literature and journalism in Europe and America, and with it all possessed of psychic gifts extraordinary.

Edwin Bjorkman says, in his "Voices of Tomorrow":

"To Francis Grierson belongs the honor of having first attained to prophetic vision of the common goal. In his first volume, published in Paris in 1889, he suggested every idea which since then has become recognized as essential not only to Bergson and Maeterlinck, but to the constantly increasing number of writers engaged in making the time conscious of its own spirit."

The messages that follow appeared in a book, printed in 1921, titled "Psycho-Phone Messages" published in Los Angeles by the Austin Publishing Company. We are indebted to the daughter of Dr. B. F. Austin for permission to reproduce them in this volume.

It is suggested that the reader note the differences in style and language of the various messages. We leave it to historians familiar with the writings of the men purporting to speak through Francis Grierson to evaluate the truth of the claims as to their source.

THE LATE GENERAL U. S. GRANT

Recorded September Ninth, 1920

The imbroglio started by President Carranza is beginning to influence the politicians of Buenos Aires and other centers in South America. They have secretly repudiated the Monroe Doctrine. Their next maneuver will be a public repudiation.

I would say to Congress, stop juggling with phrases and attend to the business of the hour. The majority has been chasing shadows in

93

a sphere of politics illumined by moonshine bottled in the Blue Ridge. I was more careful of my brand. When President Lincoln asked for the label, so he could recommend it to other generals, he was not far wrong in his surmises. It is not so much the thing as the quality that counts. Most of you at Washington will have to learn the difference between inhibition and prohibition.

The United States will be isolated within three years from this date if the blowhards from the woolly constituencies are not suppressed. You need a broncho buster in the Senate and a donkey muzzler in the House.

When a boycott is started by the countries south of the Union, your enemies in Europe will begin to act. It is not a question of commerce, but of common sense. I repeat what Lincoln said in 1862: "The times are dark and the spirits of ruin are abroad in all their power."

My message to Congress is: See that fifty thousand troops are stationed permanently near the District of Columbia.

My message to the Governors of New York, Pennsylvania and Illinois is: Get ready! The troops on the borders of Texas, New Mexico and Arizona are inadequate. The fortifications of the Panama and at San Diego and San Pedro are inadequate. You are in the same condition the French were in previous to 1789, when the motto was, "After us the Deluge." The Deluge came but it did not consist of water.

Our foes of the old Germany and the new Russia count on crippling the United States through South America, with the aid of Japan; but he who delivers the first blow will be the victor.

The Germans still believe they can eventually invade France, enter Paris and cause a revolution, found a new empire to include France, Belgium, Holland and Switzerland, with Italy later on. This dream includes a practical understanding with Soviet Russia, which, by that time, they expect would be weary of futile experiments. Plots will be exposed that will make it apparent how vain some of your optimistic surmises have been. Diplomats who are not psychologists will be balked by developments in Switzerland, that nation having become the rendezvous of disillusioned wire-pullers without a country.

You are now at the cross-roads. Take the wrong turning and you will come to the skull and cross bones.

I could say much more, but we are not yet experts in this new mode of intercommunication and must be brief.

General U. S. Grant

(Second Message)

Recorded May Third, 1921

Congress has never been so supine and so serpentine.

Millions are sent to the people of distant countries in no way related to our government or people, and yet Congress permits thousands of veterans of the great war to continue in a state of neglect, suffering and humiliation.

Do the authorities believe that when the day of trial arrives, the friends and relatives of these veterans will hurry to volunteer for active service? The country is being fascinated by incidents and events in far-off regions, and the tragic conditions at home have entered a chronic stage.

There are too many old men in Congress—, men who never did more than fight grasshoppers or watch a game of football from reserved seats.

The politicians of Buenos Ayres have now spoken as I predicted in my first message. They have attacked Mr. Harding for his speech on Pan-Americanism, all of which goes to prove that the President is repeating for South America Mr. Wilson's blunders in France.

Remember what Lincoln said to Judge Whitney:—

"Those fellows think I don't see anything, but I see all around them. I see better what they want to do with me than they do themselves."

The politicians of South America see better what the President wants to do with them than he does himself.

The administration will face a critical period in the early fall. There will be a break in the dominant phalanx. A social and political readjustment will compel mediation in the most unexpected quarters.

Thomas Jefferson

Few politicians understand the difference between scene-shifting and progress. Things shift, new names are applied, but the vicious circle continues.

I see no evidence that human nature has changed since my time, in this or any other country.

If the Republican ship of state is leaking, the Democratic craft is drifting without sail or rudder. What your statesmen fail to understand is that progress is not induced by force but by free will. New political planks rammed into your platforms against the wishes of the majority are without significance. The phrase, "The Solid South," which meant something vital at one time, has no meaning in these days of quick change and movie-show influences.

Democracy, in some sections, is a matter of climate. If you have come to a point where science and sentimentality are engaged in a drastic war, then the democratic phalanx must undergo some rude changes.

The Democratic tail wagged the Republican dog for some time, but that curious spectacle has lost its hold on public interest. It is not now a question of one end wagging the other, but who will wag both. If Republicans stand for crude force, and Democrats for ante-bellum sentimentality, both are doomed together.

In the South, Democracy means politics at the polls, aristocracy in the parlor. In the North, Republicanism means the aristocracy of wealth.

However, your conception of social equality is undergoing modification.

In Washington's time, the slogan was "revolution"; in Lincoln's time it was "abolition"; in your time it is "prohibition"; which reminds me that laws passed in haste bring long periods of repentance.

Effective effrontery is the result of courageous ignorance, for millions are more easily influenced by illusive promises than by the lessons of experience.

Modern civilization has hurried to meet four deadly things—riches, pleasures, materialism and war.

Benjamin Franklin

There is but one mark of patriotism and that is vigilance and enthusiasm. The cause of your trouble is the sincerity with which your foes think and act and the lukewarm sentiment shown by Americans. The reason is to be found in the comfort and luxury of the present day as compared with the pioneer sacrifices of your fathers and grandfathers. Your opponents are vindictive as well as vigilant. They mean what they say and do what they will. They are working as individuals, as well as in groups and parties, but Americans who inherited the land with liberty are exchanging both for the license of the law.

When the school teachers and farm hands are permitted to leave the country for the city, the end is not so far off as your sophisticated solons of the State Capitols would lead you to suppose.

I once stated that three movings equal one fire, and I can say now that the lack of teachers and farm hands has resulted in a damage equal to one revolution. No calamity comes and goes single handed. The world, the flesh and the devil are a triumvirate bound together by ties of consanguinity. Your school teachers are passing over to the world, your farm laborers to the flesh, and your ministers to the devil.

The nation will awake one day to the disillusioning fact that peace and progress can not be gauged by commercial prosperity alone. For without food, what avails your steel, your oil and your gold?

If you could witness the mortifications poor Andrew Carnegie is now undergoing because of his lack of vision, you would have a lesson not soon forgotten. He built libraries but furnished no books to fill them. It was like building houses without windows. When leading business men commit such folly what can you expect of the nation at large?

The three things most needed by the people are food, raiment and shelter. The next three are instruction, religion and discipline. Liberty is a privilege; it comes after all the others. The individual has no rights inimical to those of the collective conscience.

Until you learn this fundamental maxim, all your knowledge will prove but a sounding brass and a tinkling cymbal.

The nations are rattling over the cobble stones of bankruptcy on a buckboard of compromise, on the high road to revolution.

JOHN MARSHALL

(The Expounder of the Constitution)

Recorded October, 1920

Some recent decisions of the Supreme Court of the United States are, more than any other factor, calculated to develop and foster an element of natural unrest. Its deliberations are beyond the intelligence of many and above the interests of the majority. Its psychology is that of a divorce between capital and labor. Its rulings remind me of what transpired in England early in the nineteenth century.

Many who were not socialists are beginning to turn from the older order, imbued with the feeling that nothing could happen for the country at large, in the future, worse than the conditions that are being endured in the present.

A revolution arrives after a series of connected events which exhaust the patience of the public, and events are moving with intensity as well as rapidity.

Many of the smaller nations, instead of being content with their liberty, have thrown it away for the license that always goes with land grabbing. For a nation is nothing more than an individual with a certain amount of collective ambition.

Much of the work of the League of Nations will have to be undone. But it will not be undone by any League. The nations will settle differences in accordance with the law that permits the more powerful to wield control commensurate with their geographical and intellectual importance.

All people have rights which ought to be respected, but some have privileges as well as rights, and the privileged will hold the upper hand as long as intelligence takes precedence of illiteracy, energy dominates over lethargy, and the power of organized numbers rules over minorities.

Your statesmen and your mediators will have to learn the distinction between rights and privileges. All are supposed to possess common rights under the common law, but it is wisdom, supported by poise and power, that constitutes privilege. David and Solomon were privileged. So were Alfred the Great, Washington and Lincoln.

A nation is temperamental like an individual. The temperament may be vascillating or it may be stolid; it may be logical or it may be commercial; or a combination of the Saxon and the Celt.

The nations that will hold the balance of power in the future will be the ones with the most will and poise, backed by number. Riches alone will not save. Wealth did not save Germany from disaster, nor did it help Napoleon III to ward off the Prussian invasion in 1870. Wealth invites invasion and conquest. This is why England and America will now be the principal target for the ambitious and the discontented. This is why Japan seeks a firm foothold in China, and the Russians an entrance to India through Persia.

Without the prospects of loot there would be no war. When ambition and glory lure a nation on, the desire for loot supplies the motor force. When hunger forces a people to invade a nation, loot becomes a necessity.

What the wealthy of every nation refuse to understand, or even to consider, is that material force engenders vanity, individualism, rivalry and envy. All manifestations of force contain an element of disintegration. The type of a nation will always represent the policy and the trend of the nation.

The supreme blunder of the Peace Conference was made when the delegates, with Mr. Wilson at their head, refused to face the fact that no nation can rise above the ideals and idiosyncrasies of the national temperament, and that sudden liberation from restraint is as dangerous for a country as it is for an individual.

There is but one step between liberty and license, and that step meant pandemonium for all classes in Russia. For other peoples it may mean political bondage and the total loss of a national spirit. For the Hindoos it will mean civil wars between the different native rulers; for China, it has meant a series of revolutions and counter revolutions which may have to be suppressed by the drastic hand of a Japanese Bonaparte.

The League Conference at Versailles took no account of the working of natural law. Sentimentality was the key-note of Mr. Wilson's idealism, and commercial expansion the dominant idea of his opponents.

As for religion exerting any fundamental influence for peace and right thinking, it caused Protestants to fight Protestants and Catholics to fight Catholics, while German and Austrian cardinals did all in their power to aid in the invasion and conquest of Belgium and France on one hand, and Italy, the stronghold of the Papal See, on the other; and all this in the face of the statement of the Kaiser that Catholicism must be destroyed. Nothing like it has been known since the dawn of Christianity.

The only apparent reason for the quiescent attitude of some of the smaller nations is that they are without the material means of waging war on their neighbors.

Just as long as politicians are impelled by self-interest there will be found nations that will have to use force for the suppression of license and the curtailment of liberty. In every country the people are getting what their thoughts and deeds create for them.

Daniel Webster

You will search the pages of history in vain without finding a parallel to present conditions.

The war gave Bohemia her freedom; at the same time it licensed a Bohemian poet to keep Italy stewing in her own juice, a Bohemian journalist from New York to direct affairs in Moscow, and a Bohemian socialist from Switzerland to rule over Russia.

Added to this, a fashionable ladies' pianist has tried his hand, or should I say fingers, in the science of unfurling the sails of Poland's new Ship of State, while shop-keepers direct affairs in Germany and pusilanimous politicians keep the people in America in a state of tepid trepidation and flatulent turmoil. Can you wonder that the country is being hypnotized by the sight of so many cantankerous cataleptics?

Macbeth declared he had waded in so far that returning would be as perilous as going on. Nothing will move them until they are swamped by the high tide of reaction and flung as flotsam on the rocks of a stormy opportunism.

A new Damocles has a sword suspended over the National Capitol, and liberty hangs to the hinges of the Constitution by a hair.

Benjamin Disraeli

Some Members of Parliament have lost their reason, the majority have lost their wits, all are without vision.

Lloyd George presents the curious spectacle of a man of the people who observes them through the glasses of a Welsh Calvinist. He is a democrat with demeanor of a lord, a radical who has fallen between the two stools of the middle-class and the landed aristocracy. Nonconformist sentimentality, on one hand, and titled wealth on the other, have blinded him to the imperative needs of the time and the dangers that confront the Empire.

The English people of the past twenty years have suffered as much from misgovernment as the Germans and the Russians, but they cannot stop the present stream of progress by clatter in the House and appeals to patriotism.

For years England has been saddled with cabinets composed of professional humorists and humdrum moralists.

Augustine Birrell was a diluted edition of Sydney Smith, and Bonar Law should have been a professor of theology in a Presbyterian seminary. Sir Edward Carson played the role of an unfrocked priest in the service of the Creator. Earl Curzon is a political derelict whose presence in the Council Chamber prevents unity and impedes progress.

History will record their acts as the most amazing in the annals of Great Britain. I see nothing for the old order but unconditional surrender. The hand-writing on the wall was visible in 1909, but no preparation was made for the change which is now sweeping the country with cyclonic force.

100

We, from our side, can do no more than utter some words of warning for the few who have ears to hear, the tidal wave of change not being confined to particular countries or regions.

I, too, when Prime Minister, was blind to the reality, having been born and reared in an atmosphere as foreign to that of the masses as the atmosphere of the Winter Palace was foreign to the peasants of Russia.

We staggered under the load of a wealthy and titled upper class. They consumed the people's time and imposed infinite misery on some millions of toilers, and for these things we rewarded the men at the top with fresh titles.

As you know, I led the Conservative party in England for many years, but that party was, and still is, avid for power.

The Liberal party was made up of men using Nonconformity as an instrument of advancement. They placed opportunity above the truth, position above principle, power above progress. We were all intellectual automatons, set in motion by springs wound up by leaders who were themselves automatons.

England goes by machinery. Her very existence is mechanical. Now, when a loose screw stops the revolution of the wheels, the whole nation stops.

In what way can we be said to excel in probity of conduct the people of Ireland? In what way are we superior to Irish politicians? The scandals that occurred in London during the war would not have been tolerated in Dublin under an Irish Parliament. And still England is being led by a Welsh Calvinist, opposed by a Scottish humorist who says his prayers, backed by Anglican agnostics and middle-class dissenters overwhelmed with fear.

We always imitate the French, but while we accepted Voltairianism in principle, the French had the courage to put it into practice.

While the French became practical pagans in 1789, we became practical hypocrites.

It is this element that has created the moral indifference of the Anglican Church and the intellectual apathy of the so-called Nonconformist conscience. This is why there is no stability behind the old phraseology, the old ceremonials, the old confessions of faith—now so many catch-words which the people abhor. And this is why the working men find it so easy to send their leaders to Parliament. For the same reason Russian radicalism is certain of a warm welcome on English soil.

It is true that this hypocrisy is subconscious, having had its origin during the French Revolution. This renders it far more dangerous because political leaders in England today are mentally incompetent to realize the danger that lies before them.

We cannot reason with people whose vision is dulled by four generations of moral apathy. Hence they will continue to "kick against the pricks" to the bitter end. There will be strife added to strife, confusion to confusion, and they, themselves, will invite the drastic events which must follow so much stubborn resistance to the demands of common justice and the progress of civilization.

PRINCE BISMARCK

Recorded November 3rd, 1920

When I imposed an indemnity of five billion francs on the French people in 1870, we knew that the money could and would be paid. But there is no parallel between Germany in 1920 and France in 1870. The Reparations Commission has only succeeded in proving its incompetence. The German delegates have shown that the Allied war claims amount to more than five hundred billion marks (gold), which is nearly four thousand billions at the present rate of exchange.

This fantastic sum, one hundred times more than France paid to Germany in 1870, is expected of a country on the verge of revolution and chaos. I charge this Commission with incompetence, extravagance, luxurious living, and claims at once absurd and ridiculous.

You punish some of the most dangerous criminals by indeterminate sentences, which frequently end after a year's imprisonment, but you expect to hold the German people in financial bondage for more than a generation to come because of the criminal blunders of less than a hundred individuals.

I was blinded by material factors at the time of my seeming triumphs but now I can see some of the things which will never come to pass. The French and the English are repeating some of the blunders I made fifty years ago. They are counting on conditions which will never exist, like a bird sitting on a nest of mixed eggs from which the cuckoo will eventually oust all the other birds.

French people are under the illusion that Russia will meet the obligations undertaken by the late Czar. To expect such a thing shows the child-like illusions under which French fanatics are living. They are still wrapped in the swaddling clothes of politics.

102

We committed crimes that have brought civilization to the brink of chaos, but we are not capable of such naivete.

The logic of a Frenchman is no better than the mysticism of a Russian or the sentimentality of an Englishman. French people learned nothing from the blunders of Napoleon III and the debacle of Sedan. And the reason? They have remained provincial while the Germans imitated the commercial cosmopolitanism of the English.

Advice is the cheapest of all things. Nevertheless, I advise your statesmen to place no reliance on sentimental contracts written on paper foredoomed to become "scraps."

I do not hesitate to declare that no agreement signed since 1913 is worth more than the seals. In Europe, leaders and rulers have passed from an international game of chess to a national gamble with marked cards.

You have now to deal with an element which did not exist in my time. This element embraces all factions of the new radicalism, no matter in what country or under what leader. Some of these elements may unite, but they are not going to change. How, then, can you undertake to insure the future by contracts signed and sealed by elderly gentlemen with good intentions and poor judgment?

The war gave the new factions the long wished-for opportunity. They seized it in Russia, in Germany, in Poland, in Britain, and other countries. But the opportunities created by the war are one thing, the opportunities of tomorrow will be different, and it is this contingency for which your leaders are not prepared. You will have to select men of vision who will judge events as they arrive, without regard to the distant future, which belongs to no man.

One of my greatest mistakes was in separating Protestant Prussia from the interests of the Catholics of South Germany.

The new radicalism is opposed to some things which are irrevocably linked with religious doctrine.

Without the Catholic Church all Europe would be in the throes of the Commune. The principal cause of our disintegration was that we sanctioned Protestant flirtation with modern materialism.

France is beginning to see that even a weak monarchy is better than a radical government without a God.

You may expect a return of the monarchy in more than one country. Agnostics and Protestants, moved by fear on one side, and disgust on the other, will unite for a restoration as their last hope. There will be a repetition of historic events.

103

Bonaparte was ushered in by the French Revolution, and his advent was followed by three kings and one emperor.

The majority treat their rulers as children treat their toys: when the novelty wears off, a change is demanded.

Political psychology and religious sentiment are not the same thing. Nevertheless, they must be considered together. The Germans are not awaiting the hour when the inevitable change will be demanded. Events take crowns from some heads and place them on others. If the ex-Kaiser ever occupies the throne again, a modern Nero will fiddle amidst the ruins of German imperialism, for you know he meddled with fiddle strings as well as with political wires.

You think it strange? The impossible is always happening. Never lose sight of the fact that an organized minority is more formidable than a disorganized majority. Three men brought about the coup d'etat that placed the outcast Louis Napoleon on the throne; one man started the Russian Revolution, I planned the overthrow of the Second Empire with the aid of Count von Moltke. The majority put their trust in numbers, but the bigger a thing grows, the nearer it is to disintegration. An autocratic minority ruled in Germany, an automatic majority rules in France and England. Two men started the present rule in Moscow, both of them from the outside.

"God has been merciful to us," said Cavour, in the Italian Senate, "He has made Spain one degree lower than Italy." God has been merciful to Germany, He has made Russian communism more abhorrent than German socialism.

Nothing will be left undone by the French government to secure permanent occupation of the coal district of the Rhine.

Conditions will not remain long as they are. They are preparing decisive coups in Bavaria, Hanover, Austria, and Hungary. New combinations will amaze your statesmen and diplomats, who are ignorant of the fact that changes and upheavals operate in cycles of three and seven. What they call chance is the working of law. Spiritual forces operate through the physical, and nature will take a hand in the reactions of Petrograd and Moscow. Cold, Hunger and Starvation will dissipate the hopes of the ruling minority. Untold numbers will be sacrificed.

During the French Revolution philosophers and thinkers were decapitated. In Russia such men are killed by hunger, the difference being one of method.

Such conditions will be repeated in different countries until people learn that the spiritual cannot be separated from the material without pain and slaughter.

After all the long-winded conferences and shorthand reports, nothing is left but a confusion of blots on the tissue paper of time.

I may say more on another occasion.

Abraham Lincoln

Events come and go in cycles—there is a beginning, a middle and an end. The League of Nations had a beginning and it will have an end. But what kind of an end? Will it be one of victory or one of ignominy?

The two fatal blunders of the Kaiser and his cohorts consisted in the delusion that England could not raise, equip and transport a body of troops sufficient to offer adequate resistance to the invaders of France in conjunction with the French and Belgian armies, and that America could not or would not join the European allies.

At the present juncture the inimical forces, both in continental Europe and in America, are repeating the old blunders under fresh conditions.

History is a repetition of the old tunes with new variations. Just now the fireworks of sophistry and rhetoric drown out the familiar tune and what is heard is the buzz-saw of political machinery.

Hyenas are gnawing the bones left by the lion rampant of Czardom; and Siberia, the remnant, is being consumed by jackals from Japan. It remains to be seen how long voters with American pedigrees will be influenced by demagogues who would induce them to part with their birthright for a mess of pottage burnt on the bottom.

The longer you wink at anarchy in Europe, the greater will be the menace of social chaos at home. The worship of shibboleths cannot be kept up beyond a point where the majority grow tired of hocus-pocus politics and academical agnosticism.

There should be harmony of interests in dealing with the people of Mexico, from whom you have much to learn in many ways.

The Obregon Government should be recognized at Washington and immediate steps taken to insure cordial relations between the two countries.

The City of Mexico is a capital with a great future.

You are about to pass through a period of great confusion. Warnings have been given but not heeded. Unless you cease to theorize, and propagate a spirit of justice and judgment, the near future will develop something more than storms in the blue china teapots of diplomacy.

GENERAL BENJAMIN H. GRIERSON

1826–1911

Late Commander of the Military Department of Southern California, Arizona and New Mexico

In 1914 western civilization was threatened by a military autocracy centralized at Berlin. Europe is now threatened by a communistic tyranny centralized at Moscow and by an autocratic aristocracy centered in Japan, anti-Christian, anti-democratic, anti-American. You may call it fate or destiny, it matters not so long as you know what the signs and portents are.

We can see what is going on in the navy yards of the Nipponese Empire. We have noted the strenuous efforts put forth in naval preparations there.

A Japanese Bonaparte will soon dominate China and prevent Christian propaganda throughout Asia. I could give you the dates fixed for certain maneuvers and events in connection with Japanese ambitions relating to America, but they could change the dates. Suffice it to say they are making ready as fast as possible, much faster than many in this country could be made to believe. When this decisive moment arrives for action it will come suddenly, like the invasion of Belgium by the Germans.

Here are some of their expectations:—

The invasion of the coast of Mexico and a coalition of Japanese forces with some military faction in Mexico likely to be of practical aid, the bombing of American cities on the Pacific Coast from the air, virtual cessation of communication between certain sections east of the Rocky Mountains and California, brought about not so much by physical means as by revolutionary influences. They are counting on a Soviet revolution east of the Rockies while they are gaining a foothold in California.*

* General Grierson died in 1911. The foregoing message was received in 1920. The "Tanaka Memorial" containing the military and economic plan of world conquest since followed by Japan was not presented to the Emperor of Japan until July 25, 1927, seven years after his message from General Grierson was received.

106

One of their first attempts would be to bomb the railway passes in the Cascades and the Sierra Nevadas.

General Grant has warned you in regard to the Panama Canal and other points that need immediate attention. Millions would be alarmed if they could realize how much the Government at Washington resembles the British Government just before the German descent into Belgium. Are they waiting until they can spy the enemy through field glasses?

I could give a map of the plans of approach of the Japanese navy, intended to operate in separate units, but it would do no good. They are ready to change their tactics at any time, and have done so more than once.

Do not be surprised when I say that they proclaim the end of Christian civilization was reached when the Anglo-Saxons took possession of the Pacific Coast.

In the Far East, British domination attained its zenith in India; in America, Anglo-Saxon influence attained its limit in California. The possession of the Pacific Coast of North America is, therefore, the limit for the dominant white race. The tocsin has sounded for a Japanese avatar who will unify the political, commercial and religious forces of Japan and China, give the coup de grace to a tottering civilization and dominate the world. So do they reason and preach.

ALEXANDER HAMILTON

1757–1804

What do the clouds on the social horizon predict? Is nature a book of fate? If so, is it open or sealed? Whoever understands the political actions of the past can foresee the reactions of the future.

Human nature is always the same.

The two things brought to the surface by great upheavals are extreme virtues and extreme vices. The virtues of self sacrifice, on the one hand, the vice of self interest on the other. Vice is flexible, cunning, adaptable.

You are living at a time when profiteers amaze by their cynical audacity, but profiteers have always existed. Before the war the nobles of Russia and Germany were profiteers in landed privileges and governmental perquisites. The tillers of the soil were free in name, serfs in practice. In England two or three hundred lords and peers

107

possess the land. In America food profiteering began during the Civil War. This national vice has never been attacked at the roots.

Your age is characterized by a high level of predatory ability and a low level of prophetic visibility.

The old hackneyed phrase, "This is a free country," has been applied in varying degrees according to the caprice of the individual with the most aggressive will.

New words, definitions, excuses, have been invented to meet the new conditions, but of all the words yet brought into use, "camouflage" is the only one that covers the cynical effrontery of predatory hypocrisy. It is a vocable of universal utility. It applies to the cockpits of commerce as well as to the arena of bull and bear politics.

It depicts a Hindoo patience in the pulpit and a Hoodoo palsy in the pews.

The word "democracy" itself is the stripes painted on the sides of the old Ship of State in her zigzag course to elude the torpedoes of the proletarian submarines.

A capitalistic profiteer is a highbrow optimist who lives by the sweat of the lowbrow pessimist. The stretching process will cease suddenly like the snapping of a rubber stretched beyond the limit.

The masses without a voice always find articulation in the unlooked-for man, the unlooked-for group.

The people without a mouthpiece are a mob, and no mob can run itself for more than a few days. It is the initiated who lead, and leadership requires time, patience, judgment.

In the world of genius there are no upstarts.

The great leader never rises suddenly. Bonaparte was a military graduate, Grant was a product of West Point, Lincoln was thirty years preparing for the Presidency, Lenin spent twenty years in the study of economics. All countries have the same experience.

Voltaire endowed the middle classes of France with a voice, united the disaffected of all classes, and peppered their indignation with pungent epigrams. He created an intellectual garden for lovers of liberty, and from the realm of the mind flung the thorns of ridicule in the face of titled imbeciles and crowned the heads of scholars with laurel.

The people of France were washed by Louis XIV, wrung by Louis XV, and dried in the back yard of tyrannical economics by Louis XVI.

But it was the orators and pamphleteers who ironed out the frills and furbelows of the old order.

108

The foregoing messages were recorded during the year 1920. The following messages were recorded almost two decades later, during the latter months of 1939.

We are indebted to Jocelyn Pierson, editor, and the Board of Trustees for permission to reprint the following "War Prophecies" which first appeared in the October, 1939, number of the *"Journal of the American Society for Psychical Research."*

The questions were spoken aloud to the medium. The answers were received through the automatic writing of Mrs. Ebling, a young, non-professional medium. The prophecies purport to be those of William James and F. W. H. Myers, both deceased and in control of the hand of Mrs. Ebling.

William James (1842–1910) was a distinguished American philosopher and professor of psychology at Harvard from 1881 to the time of his death. He was the outstanding psychologist of his day and the author of several books on psychology and philosophy. He was interested in psychical research and was one of the pioneers in that field.

Frederick W. H. Myers (1843–1901) was one of the founders of the Society of Psychical Research. Among the many books that he wrote during his life is "Human Personality, Its Survival of Bodily Death." First published in 1900 this famous study of clairvoyance, telepathy and related phenomena has been reprinted this year by Longmans.

It is natural that both of these men, interested as they were in psychical research, should maintain contact with our world through the mediums investigated by the Society. The messages were automatically written on March 20, 1939. Hitler had just taken Czechoslovakia and Roumania, and the European situation had been depressing Miss Pierson, who asked the questions. The replies are quoted from the original manuscript and are unaltered and unedited.

We are indeed blessed by the sphere of life to which God has committed us. We know of the chaos you are facing in your world. Life is so ephemeral it is over almost before we are aware of its implications on earth. That is why we need all of eternity to complete tasks to which we had dedicated ourselves. Our work here is in part a work of earth, since there is a constant interflow of ideas. It is only in this way that progress can be made on earth. This is the explanation of the constantly evolving universe of mind and matter.

Question: Is it true that Hitler is a medium in the hands of lower forces?

This is very true. That is why he must be alone so much. He receives direct guidance from powers who are diabolical. Remember the analogy of the temptation of our Lord when he was taken in spirit to the top of the mountain and offered all the kingdoms of the world if he would but yield allegiance to the Tempter. Hitler has a group of mystics with him who are in touch with powerful lower forces. He is forewarned in this way of moves made against him and of the best time to stage his coups.

Question: Is it also true, as Chamberlain has been said to believe, that he is inspired by the angels?

This I do not believe. He is a very astute politician whose angelic voice is the voice of his own conscience which has been conditioned by his loyalty to the imperial vested interests and the empire in general.

Question: Do you think that when the showdown comes, England and France will have a dog's chance?

The whole setup is now definitely to the advantage of the totalitarian states. They are now in control of strategic places and control vast sources of raw materials which formerly they did not have. Their air equipment alone is quite sufficient to blow up most of the cities of France and England and in very quick order. The democracies could now be quickly cowed by this superior air force. Hitler is just biding his time to strike.

Question: Will it come this year?

No, the time is not ready. First the easterly advance and then the western.

Question: Won't England and France be better able to defend themselves by then? Have they become soft?

The democracies move too slowly. There is dissension of class and caste within the ranks so that a united movement for an offensive defense is not possible. They are being trapped by stupidity; pride in their ancient sovereignty, and in the unrealistic attitude which they have taken to Hitler in the past. It is almost too late now.

Question: What will happen? Will Germany dominate the world?

No, it is deeper than that. It is a battle not only of nations but of ideas. There will be fire and blood and steel. There will be marching feet and droning motors. There will be darkness and horror all over the civilized world before this thing is settled.

Question: How many years will it take us to come through this and how much involved will this country be?

Within five years the fire will be raging. The conflagration will leap from ocean to ocean, from nation to nation, and the struggle will not be confined to the great powers. *It will be fought as class against class and brother against brother.*

Question: Is this the coming of the anti-Christ prophesied by the biblical books before the Second Coming of the Messiah?

This period strangely does correspond to all the signs and portents which have been predicted but no man can say when the Son of Man will appear. Only the Supreme One who is within and about all that exists has knowledge of when the Messiah will appear.

Question: Do you really think we will work into a more spiritual age within our lifetimes or must we go through another "Dark Ages"?

These are "Dark Ages." The period which is to follow will be as much more spiritual as this period is in comparison with medieval times. We are fighting to emerge but the forces of evil are arrayed against this flowering of divine hope and are trying to destroy the work of centuries of Christian Teaching.

Question: Give us an answer to the age-old and perhaps foolish question: Why is there evil?

If there was no evil, where would the good be? There would be no basis for comparison. If there was no resistance,—no friction, there would be no laws of physics. Light is created from darkness. Matter is created from the void.

Question: Will we live to see the dawning of this new day?

You are within the dawning even as you are on the threshold of the destruction of the things which have kept men in slavery these centuries as well as opposing forces for good.

Question: May we ask you if the war will last a long time?

There will be one war after another until the causes of war have been eliminated. This will probably be of a long duration.

Question: I've always understood that war really never did away with the causes of war.

There will be compromise, concessions, education, martyrdom of apostles of peace and a realization of the eventual necessity for some other solution to the difficulties which exist between rival powers.

Question: I have always advocated a true Socialism, though doubt the practicability of it because of the lack of spiritual and intellectual equality. Is there going to be an enlightened Socialism in this country as a result of class strife, or a tyrannical collectivism?

Before the Utopia can materialize, you will probably get a very bad form of dictatorship here due to war conditions.

April 11, 1939.

(It will be remembered that Mussolini moved into Albania on April 7, 1939.)

Question: What shall it be—Europe or closer to home?

Whatever you choose.

Allow us to present a lugubrious essay entitled "The Betrayal of

112

Democracy." If you will recall, three years ago Myers wrote to you in Hyslop House that it would be three years before the war broke and that it would begin in the Balkans. This war has now begun. The opening guns have not yet been fired by the British but the time is due when the policy pursued by Chamberlain can no longer be maintained. The interests of the Empire are now being threatened by the Fascist government.

* * *

England, America and France have sown the wind. Soon they will reap the whirlwind. There is no issue which has arisen that they could not have foreseen months—yes—even years ago. However, in the name of democracy, they have doomed democracy. What recognition did they give to the embryonic democracy which had been formulated in Germany after the Versailles treaty? They killed this democracy by hatred and unfair policies. The flower of democracy blossomed in Spain. Inspired by the example of the larger democracies, the people of Spain formed a republic.

Oh, democracies of America, Britain and France,—you were guilty of the death of this democracy when, like the priests and levites of old, you refused assistance to the broken and bleeding republic that looked to you for aid. For the wanton betrayal of Czechoslovakia, we know that before the highest tribunal of justice you are indicted.

Other democracies are nearly extinct. France is reaping her reward. Her own democracy is finished. England is no longer lighted by the sacred glow of democratic principle, and we, in America, for the sin of stupidity and selfishness will pay with our liberties for the violation of our sacred responsibilities.

Question: I call this a hymn of failure and do not agree with you anyway about the Spanish Republic—a lot of Communists really.

We will not quibble now. That is not the issue. The issue is the death of democracy as we have known it. Out of the ashes of that which is to come may emerge a world purified by suffering and more receptive to the ideals of Christianity, which are in the last analysis the only foundation for lasting peace and a benevolent government by the people and for the people.

April 17, 1939.

Question: What do you think of the world situation and Roosevelt's speech?

It is one of the most courageous acts of statesmanship that has ever been voiced in our country. In the present state of world affairs, England and France are no longer able to cope with the dictator powers alone.

Question: Do you think it will do any good?

In the long run, yes. In the immediate situation—no. The dictators are on the march. They will brook no interference. Their present indecision is largely because of public sentiment in their home fields. Seeds of revolt have been sown against their ruling classes which will eventually react strongly to weaken their regimes.

Question: When you wrote that democracy was doomed, did you mean the democracies hadn't a chance of winning a war against the dictators, or that democratic government would be superseded by dictatorship in the now democratic countries?

Nowhere in the world does real democracy exist now. Certain northern countries have an approximate condition—Sweden, Norway and Denmark—since their rulers are nominal in their functioning. Britain and France are now democratic in name only. If a war— and by "if" I mean when a war does come, dictatorial powers will be granted to the nation's head that will invest him with powers which will limit democratic procedure to such an extent that we shall no longer have the right to regard America as a true democracy.

Question: That is bad, but not as bad as the meaning I thought you suggested.

You thought of the forcible overthrow of the present government?

Question: No, I thought perhaps the dictator countries would succeed in completely conquering the world.

Which, if you will analyze the above statement, is what I meant.

Question: Fascism may become universal but if not all dictated by Hitler and Mussolini, may not prove the same aggressive barbarism it now is. In any case, Fascism by Americans would be more bearable for Americans than control by Germans.

It is not the Germans whom we have to fear.

Question: Who is it—ourselves?

No, the Spanish Republic which has been overcome and is now

114

controlled by Franco. The plan is this in brief: There is a well-organized program which has been formulated these three years past. Franco by the help of Germany and Italy is to control Spain. Spain has an ancient claim upon many of the territories which are included in the American scheme of things: Mexico, South America, Porto Rico, Cuba and the southern part of the United States itself. Franco hopes by the help of his allies to win these territories for Spain.

Question: Then Franco is a fiercer dictator than any of them?

No—not necessarily. It is a matter of economic necessity. They are all hungry for land. The Germans are paving the way by their penetration of South America, where they hope to become powerful enough to support Franco's claim by the weight of their aircraft and eventually the sabotage of the Panama Canal.

Question: Do you think they are likely to realize such a plan especially after the Pan-American Congress?

Unless America awakens to the danger which lies ahead, there is great likelihood that she will fall into the trap set by the dictators. Roosevelt sees this peril clearly.

Question: But surely all Europe will have to be conquered by them first?

Separate—divide—then conquer. Class against class—nation against nation. They will follow and like the birds of prey that they are, devour the carrion.

Question: Well it's a depressing picture. Then you see us actually invaded in the United States?

Eventually—yes.

Question: And you still think it will not start this year?

I made no such statement—I said that it has already started. Why else should Roosevelt have interceded? The handwriting is on the wall. No shots were fired over Czechoslovakia. For the sins of selfishness and greed and isolationist policy the retribution will be dear.

Question: You see us conquered and beaten?

No, we will not be conquered but we will pay in tears and blood, steel and fire for our stupidity and greed.

115

Question: Do you think we will learn anything by it? Do people ever learn anything collectively?

If you recall the pages of your ancient history and compare the consciousness of say, the medieval period with our own, you will be able to realize the superiority of the present age in the higher forms of mental and spiritual life. It is vastly improved in its humanitarian principles—in its acceptance of scientific discoveries—in its attitudes toward women, children and the dependents of all classes. The collective conscience of civilization is now much more sensitive to the hurts and wrongs of the depressed minorities.

CHAPTER VIII

DEATH CYCLE OF AMERICAN PRESIDENTS

PROPHECY OR COINCIDENCE

By a strange coincidence, beginning with 1840 and every twentieth year, every man elected to the American presidency IN A YEAR ENDING IN A ZERO was either ASSASSINATED or otherwise DIED IN OFFICE. In other words, the president elected in 1840, and the one elected in every twentieth year thereafter, was prevented by DEATH, either natural or violent, from COMPLETING HIS TERM OF OFFICE. The presidents, with the dates of their elections, are as follows:

President	Elected	Took Office	Died	
Harrison	1840	1841	1841	
Lincoln	1860	1861	1865	(assassinated)
Garfield	1880	1881	1881	(assassinated)
McKinley	1896–1900	1897	1901	(assassinated)
Harding	1920	1921	1923	
Roosevelt	1940	?	?	

Garfield died 16 years after Lincoln.
McKinley died 20 years after Garfield.
Harding died 22 years after McKinley.
Roosevelt ? ? ? ? Harding?

By counting the terms beginning with 1865, you will find that death came to every fifth one. The presidential term of 1940–44 is the fifth term since Harding.

Many prophecies point to F. D. Roosevelt as the *last*

president under our present form of government. He will be followed by a Fascist dictator. The prophecy of Lincoln will be fulfilled by the destruction of the republic during the years 1941–45.

This destruction is well under way. The United States is already a semi-Fascist government.

CHAPTER IX

Edward Bellamy's Prophecy of a New America

Bellamy's Prophecy for America

In the year 1850, at Chicopee Falls, Mass., was born one of America's greatest prophets, Edward Bellamy. His two best known prophecies are embodied in *"Looking Backward,"* published in 1888, and *"Equality"* published ten years later. Both books have been translated into many languages and reproduced in Braille. Over fifty years ago Edward Bellamy, with illumined prophetic vision, foretold the discoveries of modern science and traced the development of capitalism. With amazing accuracy he described the radio and television; pictured our modern concentration of wealth with its accompanying dispossession of the American people. With even greater spiritual foresight, he pictured the society of the future when mankind shall have solved this paradox of want in the midst of plenty.

Bellamy had gotten started successfully on a literary career as a short story writer, and the origin of *"Looking Backward"* was to have been simply another novelette with its characters and scenery located in some fictitious land; but this story gripped the author himself as something worth serious thought. At the time, *"Das Kapital,"* by Karl Marx, was becoming popular and Bellamy, impressed by his own vision, spent nearly a year studying Marx's ponderous book; then he felt the urge to re-write and expand *"Looking Backward"* as an American brand of economics adapted wholly to our United States thinking and conditions.

The book soon became a "best seller," and, beginning in Boston, Mass., in a vacant business building loft on State Street, within a stone's throw of the Stock Exchange, a group of some twenty of Boston's literary and artistic people gathered to meet Bellamy and to organize the "First Nationalist Club." These clubs soon spread throughout the nation, mostly in the eastern section. Their development led to publishing *"The New Nation,"* of which Bellamy was editor.

The work of Epic, the Utopian Society, Technocracy, the Townsend Old Age Pension, Ham and Eggs, Money Reform, and several other organizations, are all based upon principles promulgated by Bellamy; and Franklin Roosevelt's *"Looking Forward"* seems to be a re-statement, in the light of recent economic and political developments, of the political economy first visioned by Bellamy.

At the time *"Looking Backward"* was written, the great corporations of today were in their infancy. Monopoly was still a development of the future, and while there were several rich men, there were none who ever dreamed of a million dollar yearly income. The corporate state was unheard of by the general run of mankind, and it was assumed that the age of absolute monarchs was long since past. The terms Nazism and Fascism had not been coined, and communism had an entirely different meaning in the minds of the public than it has today.

When it is remembered that Bellamy first published

his remarkable prophecy over fifty years ago, and that everything pictured in his books is now in process of fulfillment, how can one doubt the validity of his vision of the future?

Bellamy predicted that by the year 2000 the United States would be a democratic corporate state conducted for the benefit of the citizenry as a whole rather than for the benefit of the House of Have.

The growth of monopoly was foretold where giant corporations would operate in their various fields, each having a virtual monopoly. Today the entire electrical industry is controlled by A. T. & T., General Electric, Westinghouse Electric, and Radio Corporation. All of these are more or less tied in together through their banking affiliates and by their licensing arrangements of patents. Theirs is a complete monopoly. Motion pictures are a monopoly enjoyed by eight major producers who control the field through their Producers' Association. Petroleum products and the prices for which they sell, are under the dominance of Standard Oil, and so it goes in every industry.

In Germany, Italy, and the U. S. S. R. the various corporations have been taken over and combined into a super-corporation which is the state itself. The so-called democratic countries, with the start of the second world war, have become virtual dictatorships and are fast assuming the form of the corporate state. Plans are formed and laws drawn that will place industrial control of the United States in the hand of the President, who will become a dictator the minute the United States is at war.

Another prediction of Bellamy's is that the present

money system will be abolished, and a system of international planned economy will come into existence wherein there will be barter, or exchange of surpluses between various nations. Germany has long been out of gold and has been using a system of barter for some years. With Brazil she bartered manufactured products for coffee, and traded this coffee to Sweden for her products. The United States and England made a deal whereby we trade cotton for rubber. The gold standard and international finance are not going to break down. They *have* broken down, and long ago ceased to fill the requirements of the Kosmon New Era.

Bellamy stated that the new government will have control of youth for a period of three years, during which time our young men will do the general work of the country, such as conservation, road building, and reforestation.

With the introduction of the C. C. C. and the new camps now being formed, this prediction is well on the way to fulfillment. Four million youths from every state in the union are already being supervised by the National Youth Administration.

Another of Bellamy's predictions is: At the age of twenty-one the citizen is to be free to choose his vocation, is to work until he is forty-five, when he will be retired, and will thereafter be free either to loaf or pursue any line of research or hobby to occupy his time.

The many pension plans started in various states have already forced the old-age pension. With the growth of a planned economy the amount of retirement pensions will be increased and the age of retirement lowered. It has long been difficult for men over forty years of age to find work.   If industry will not employ them, then a sufficient pension must be allowed these men.

The state of the future will see to it that every able-bodied citizen is a producer and is well paid.   Dictatorships have done away with unemployment in their various countries, but will not be able to give their people decent living standards so long as their economy is planned for war.   A planned production will be the order of the new state wherein there will be plenty for all and no wasted surplus.   The efforts towards a normal granary of the Department of Agriculture are first steps in this direction.

The evidence is conclusive that every prediction of Bellamy's will be fulfilled long before the year 2000.

But even Bellamy implied a revolution.   In his book he speaks of the people living in 2000 A.D. being ignorant of the unemployment, poverty, ill-health, scarcity, warfare, and friction of yesterday and today—*for the histories and records of our times had been destroyed!* How and why would such records be destroyed other than by a national upheaval aimed at the destruction of all property records and prevailing laws?

CHAPTER X

JOHN BALLOU NEWBROUGH, AMERICA'S GREATEST PROPHET

THE GREATEST PROPHET OF THEM ALL

John Ballou Newbrough
1827–1891

On June 5, 1827, there was born at Mohickinsville, Ohio, a man who is destined to go down in history as one of the great prophets of the nineteenth century—John Ballou Newbrough.

Even when a child, John possessed remarkable clairvoyant and clairaudient faculties which he had inherited from his mother. In later life he used to laugh as he recalled an incident that happened when he was only five years old.

A piece of farm machinery had been broken while he was in town with his father who, upon his return, demanded to know which of the boys had done the mischief. Little John, hardly more than a baby, piped up, naming the guilty brother and explained just how the accident had occurred. The father told him he couldn't have seen this happen as John maintained, as he had been with him all day. But John persisted that he had seen it, and those being the days of stern fathers and old-fashioned spankings, John got his—for "story-telling."

Throwing himself down at the foot of a tree, he wept bitterly, for he knew an injustice had been done, and it was here his mother came to console him. She believed him, for she, too, possessed the faculty of seeming to be somewhere and seeing all that went on even when her body was far distant. She explained to the little fellow that this faculty of "second-sight" was usually disbelieved by those who did not possess it, and told him that unless he wished to be thought a great liar, he must be discreet and keep his strange experience to himself. This advice from his mother John never forgot. During his later years, the elder Newbrough himself became a good medium, and the link between father, mother, and son became one of perfect understanding.

John Newbrough went to the school taught by his father, and then went away to college. Forced to work his way through, he lived in a dentist's home and assisted him while he studied medicine. He was thus able, when he was graduated, to get degrees in both medicine and dentistry.

When the gold rush to California came in 1849, John Newbrough joined the trek westward and managed to amass a fortune running into five figures. He then went to the gold fields of Australia, where he collected more gold.

He next decided he had enough to "travel and see the world," which he did for several years. He "went everywhere," as he used to say himself, and crossed the ocean twice in a sailing vessel.

Returning to America, he practiced medicine in Kentucky, and for about two years was assistant doctor in an asylum for the insane. This painful experience, together with obstetrics which, as a general physician, he had to practice, caused him to abandon medicine and take up dentistry. He went to New York City, established himself as a dentist and developed a very successful practice.

It would be wrong to accuse him of "wanderlust." He did travel extensively, often living for quite a period in a place he found interesting, but the urge to travel came from a deep, inner craving to know the heart of humanity.

He wanted to know people and find out what they were like. He asked himself: "Was the man with the yellow skin so very different from his white brother?"

He sought the answer, and out of his world-wide travels he returned with the solid, practical conviction of the brotherhood of man.

Many subscribe to this in theory, but to John Newbrough it was a conviction, and he practiced it to the extent that the blackest negro was as much his brother as the fairest Anglo-Saxon; and the child of the lowest origin as much to be esteemed as the child of a royal prince. Perhaps the reason John Newbrough is to be classed among the great prophets is due to his absolute sincerity.

Coupled naturally with great humanitarian instincts was his thirst for knowledge, and the many books in his splendid library (composed entirely of non-fiction works) with their many markings and notations, bear testimony that he was a scholar of no mean ability.

He came finally, through travel and study, to that point in his search for wisdom where he craved for more knowledge than the works of man provided, and so he began the study of spirit phenomena.

Spiritualism as we now know it was then young but growing fast in the country. It was a topic of almost general interest. The intelligentsia of that day had taken it up, and the orthodox churches feared it greatly, for thousands were leaving their folds for this new faith. It became very popular, for it offered consolation to all who mourned, taught that the departed were not dead, but only changed in form, that they were still with their loved ones, still able to hear and to help and comfort those left behind on earth. It was a beautiful teaching, and people rushed to it as they had rushed for gold in California a few years before. And even as the adventurous John had been caught up in that other rush, so now he was caught up in this later one.

Born of a medium mother, and himself a medium, it was not strange to him, but the phenomena claimed by the many mediums who suddenly sprang up all over the world did challenge his reason. His mediumship was really remarkable. He could see the departed, view people and things in distant places, and he could hear in the same way. It was possible for him to hold a sealed letter in his hand and read it word for word. He could read thought. When he sat in "circles," his hands would, as he expressed it, "fly around in tantrums," often writing messages.

But these things were very different from *materializations*, the voices in the unseen made audible for all to hear, the passing of solid bodies through solid walls, and all the various manifestations of the seemingly impossible which mediums were claiming to make.

Characteristically, he was curious; he determined to find out for himself how many of these claims could be true, and again, characteristically, he made his search thorough. He not only went to see the most famous mediums in America, he brought many of them, one at a time, to live right in his own home. When this was done, he paid them well and got them to devote themselves exclusively to his investigations and experiments.

As he well knew, mediumship, in its very nature, lends itself to fraud more than any other one thing. As soon as spiritualism and mediums became so popular, the horde of charlatans sprang up with countless varieties of hoax and fraud. He only brought those to his home who were first class, reputable mediums, who had attracted the attention of serious, earnest men everywhere, in Europe as well as in America.

Having satisfied himself as to the character of the medium, he explained the purpose of his investigation. He would explain that with the medium in his house there could be no question of false floors, trap doors, trick paraphernalia. With his own hands he would put a medium into a cabinet he had himself made, and nail her gown to the floor as an extra precaution. He tested everything that was to be used in the experiment; in this setting of his own making, the medium was bound to be proven genuine or otherwise.

He continued these investigations for two years and experimented with dozens of mediums during this time. They could, he was finally led to admit, perform all the miraculous things claimed for and by them, and he was joined in this conclusion by the leading scientists of America, England, Germany, France, and Italy. He was still not satisfied. The intelligence of these spirit visitors varied from ordinary to low; their discourses were of trivial matters. He wanted to know about man, his destiny, facts about the universe, man's life after so-called death, etc.

Convinced that there must be some means whereby one could communicate with the great minds in higher worlds, provided the proper conditions were complied with, Dr. Newbrough determined to qualify himself to deserve the interest of the great spiritual immortals. For a ten-year period of development and purification he governed his thought, actions, and diet according to the Essene system. He rose every morning at sunrise and bathed. He tried to dismiss all thought of personal self, while at all times thinking of others kindly and generously. His diet was not only a strictly vegetarian one, but he also gave up drinking or using milk, eggs, and all things which developed within the soil, such as potatoes, eating only such foods as grew high up in the sunshine, as fruit and nuts.

In a brief account of himself, he tells that after he had undergone this training, a new form of control came upon him—that in place of hands being held above his hands, a light struck them when he would write, and he would not know a word he was writing until he read it later. He also became a trance medium; that is, he would go under "control" and give long and beautiful lectures or discourses. Sometimes these related to higher heavens, and sometimes they were prophecies.

Those who heard him said these lectures were never to be forgotten. He lectured for several years, sometimes as himself, and sometimes under control in various spiritualist camp-meetings, and also in New York City.

It was during part of this time that the voice which had become his tutor and guide, instructed him to purchase a typewriter, an instrument which, at that time, had just been invented and put on the market. After obtaining the typewriter, he was told to rise at dawn and sit before it, whereupon his hands would type out questions and answers relative to the earth, heaven, and the universe that no human source could answer.

It was at this point, Dr. Newbrough tells, that a new control came upon his hands. "Rays of light like wires coming through the window" fell upon the backs of his hands as he held them on the key-board. When perfection of control had been obtained, the immortals of the higher heavens of the earth were ready to transmit, through the instrumentality of Newbrough, a new spiritual document to serve humanity of the new era.

The manuscript thus given humanity is a history of our planet since its nebulous days, and of humanity since the creation of the first man on earth. It gives an account of the relationship ever existing between the unseen realms of spirit, which is the field of causes, and the seen environment, which is the region of effects. Also included in this remarkable manuscript is a detailed account of the spiritual forces instrumental in the founding of our own United States and its Constitution, the place America occupies in the transition period of today, and the Golden Age of tomorrow, a picture of the method whereby peace will replace war throughout the world.

These writings also contained a scientific section from which Albert Einstein is purported to have received the information which led to the mathematical equations substantiating the truth of relativity, the curvature of space, lens effect of a planet's atmosphere, unity of energy and matter, and other scientific statements. These scientific principles are all to be found in the Newbrough manuscripts.

Not the least important of the transcriptions is the history of an ancient school of wisdom dating back nine thousand years. Masonry is but one of this school's many manifestations.

In evaluating the prophecies that follow, quoted from these manuscripts of the Essenes, the reader should remember that the manuscript purports to have been given to men of Kosmon * at the command of the chief executive of our planet (God), and state His intentions relative to the future of the race and world.

The Future of Religion

Think not, O man, I am insufficient to these times and seasons or say that God spake in the dark days of the earth, but latterly holdeth His tongue.

Behold, I am thy elder brother, a captain of the earth and her heavens for a season. As I am, so were my predecessors in the time of the ancients.

Ambassadors of the Most High, Jehovah, the Creator.

Whose power and wisdom are given unto me, even after the same manner as are Thy earthly governments ruled and disciplined.

Whereby order may contribute to the advancement of all His created beings.

* Kosmon is a three thousand year cycle which began A.D. 1848.

My light is not to one people only. In my sight the nations of the divisions of the earth are as one people only, brothers and sisters.

I take from them their idols, their gods; but I give them a greater, even the Creator.

I suffered my children to have idols; but now, that ye are men, put away your idols and accept Jehovah who is Creator of all.

Nor shall any man more say: "I worship the Brahman principle, or the Buddhist principle or the Confucian principle, or the Mohammedan principle, or the Christian principle." For all of these have proven themselves to result in war and destruction.

None of them have faith in their Creator, but faith in their armies of soldiers and in their weapons of death.

But I give unto all people one principle only which is to serve Jehovah. This is broad enough for all men.

The War of Armageddon will destroy man's faith in Mohammedanism, Buddhism, Brahmanism, and Christianity with their harvests of death. With the acceptance of the one God, Creator of heaven and earth, unity of government and economics will follow unity of religion. Peace on earth, good will to man, will then be the order of the day, with abundant life for all.

A religion of work, rather than words, is forecast in the following:

Your temples and churches and meeting-houses shall be turned into consultation chambers to find remedies against poverty, crime and debauchery. The congregations shall be enrolled and, at the meetings, they shall be enquired after to see if they are in need. And they shall have volunteers who shall go about seeking out the helpless and distressed. Instead of the congregations listening to sermons they shall become co-workers for relief.

Let this be a prophecy to you of the words of your God. There is no such congregation this day (1881) in all the world; and yet, ere this generation pass away, this shall be proven to you.

REVOLUTION

Neither shall any king, nor queen nor any other ruler in all the world impress as a soldier any man who is unwilling to engage in war.

132

And whosoever does not obey this judgment shall be earthbound as long as war remains on earth.

Neither will I more consider the prayers of any king or queen or any ruler of any nation or people in all the world who engage in war, offensive or defensive, or who aid or abet war in any way whatsoever.

But I will abandon all such people and my Lords shall abandon them and my holy angels shall abandon them.

And they shall be afflicted with assassinations and intriguers and despoilers, and with anarchy and riots and destruction.

For they shall be made to understand that whomsoever Jehovah created alive is sacred upon the earth; and that whosoever heedeth not these, my judgments, sinneth against the Almighty.

Behold, thy God hath come to put away old things and to answer thy prayer, Thy kingdom come on earth as it is in heaven.

World Unity

In Kosmon I come saying, "Be ye brethren upon the earth and upon the waters of the earth; these are the legacies I bequeath my children. Instead of making laws against thy brother, thou shalt throw open the place of thy habitation, and receive him with open arms.

"I will have all the ports open and free, nor shall there be partisan taxation in favor of one nation against another.

"All governments are tending towards oneness with one another. This is the march of Jehovah. None can stay Him.

"Behold, a new time is in the world; from the acquisition of knowledge a new liberty hath been born into the world. It crieth out on every side: Throw open the doors unto all trades and occupations: behold, the multitude are sufficiently wise to judge themselves whom they shall patronize. Judgment is rendered against the laws and governments of man in all cases where they prevent the liberty of choice of man to his vocation and knowledge.

"In Kosmon, man shall no longer be driven in yoke and harness; he shall stand upright before his creator, practising his highest light with rejoicing, being a free man and a brother to his God."

A New Day

God saith, "Behold the work of my hand, O man; as thou findeth an old house, no longer habitable, thou sendest workmen to pull it down, (Hitler is such a workman.) and, then, thou sendest laborers to clear away the rubbish. Afterward thou sendest builders, and they lay a new foundation, larger and broader than the old one, and thereon they build a new edifice adapted with new improvements unto the increase and requirements of thy family.

"Even so hath God labored for hundreds of years to prepare unto the generations of this day.

"For I saw beforehand that man would circumscribe the earth, and that all nations and peoples would become known to one another."

"And I beheld also that in the coming time, which is now at hand, the old edifices of doctrines and creeds and religions—Brahmans, Buddhists, Jews, Confucians, Mohammedans and Christians—would not fulfill the requirements of man.

"And now, behold, O man, the wisdom of Jehovah previously. He had permitted corruptions and contradictions to creep into sacred books of all the said great religions, purposely and with design, so as to make easy the work of thy God.

"And when I saw that the coming together of nations and peoples would require a new religious edifice, I perceived, also, that the old ones must be cleared away.

"And behold, I, thy God, went to work systematically, inspiring man to accomplish even what man hath accomplished.

"I raised up scholars and infidels against these religions, inspiring them to attack the corruptions and contradictions in the sacred books of all peoples. In the same time that I sent infidels against the Jewish Bible, I sent infidels against the Hindu Bibles, and against the doctrines of Brahma and Buddha and Confucius, and the Christians and the Mohammedans.

"And I made the beginning of the work of these infidels and scholars to correspond with the discovery of America by Columbus, and I kept them at their work for three hundred years, which was up to the time of the establishment of the Republic, which I, thy God, provided to be untrammelled by an established religion. For I will have none worshipped but Jehovah.

"Only by harmony and the union of many can any great good come unto the generations of men.

"Into thy hands, O man, I give the key to peace and plenty. Remember the password which admitteth thee to the all-highest kingdoms is—Jehovah, the I AM."

Because I called and ye came not; because ye said: Thy Kingdom
come on earth as it is in heaven, and put not forth a hand in My
behalf;

Because ye saw the multitude going after intoxicating drink and
smoke and opium;

Because ye rose up not, saying: Stay thy hand, satan;

But shirked, granting licenses unto these sins;

And ye have become a polluted people;

Given to drunkenness and to smoking and to all manner of dis-
sipation;

Each one casting the blame on others, and hiding himself in self-
righteousness;

Thus opening the doors of your houses of debauchery as a temptation to the young;

Behold I am risen in judgment against you.

My holy angels I shall withdraw from your cities;

And from your places of worship;

And from your government, and your law makers and rulers;

For they have profaned me.

Making laws and granting licenses to carry on evils, knowingly and
willfully, for policy's sake;

Hoping for personal favour and gain;

For they knew that what was not good for one person was not
good for a nation;

And that whatever sin indulged in, would, sooner or later, bring
its own punishment.

And they said: We derive a large revenue from the duties and
licenses for these iniquities!

Thus hoping to justify themselves by compounding themselves.

And I said unto them: A revenue thus received shall be expended
in prisons and alms-houses, and shall not be sufficient.

Because ye granted licenses and polluted the people, behold, the
pollution shall more than balance the revenues.

The criminals and paupers shall be a greater burden than though
ye received no revenue.

Behold I showed unto you that as an individual could not sin
against Me without, soon or late, becoming answerable to Me, I
showed ye also that the same responsibility and result would befall
a nation or a people in like manner.

For which reasons, and because of your evasions of My Commandments, I called unto My God and Lords and My Holy Angels, saying; Waste not your time and labour more with the worldly;

Nor answer ye their prayers when they call on My Name;

For they have become a conceited people, saying: There is no God and Jehovah is as void as the wind.

Behold ye shall let them go their way; their cities shall become full of crime, for angels of darkness shall come amongst them, and no city shall be safe from theft, murder and arson.

And vagabonds shall travel in the country places, stealing and robbing and murdering.

And their great men shall take bribes, and their judges shall connive with sin; and the innocent shall be confined in mad-houses.

And justice shall depart away from them.

The employee shall pilfer and steal from his employer; and the employer shall hire others to look after those in his employee.

But all things shall fail them.

For I will make them understand that I am the first principle in all things;

And that I am justice;

And that I am purity;

And that whoso raise a hand against justice, purity, virtue, wisdom and truth also raiseth his hand against Me.

I made the way of life like going up a mountain; whoso turneth aside and goeth downward shall ultimately repent of his course, and he shall retrace his steps.

To a nation and a people and a government of a people, I am the same.

Righteousness shall be first and foremost of all things.

Their governors and lawmakers shall be made to know this.

When they were a monarchy, I held the king responsible.

But when I gave unto the multitude to govern themselves, behold, I gave also responsibility unto them.

And they sought not to make laws for righteous government unto the whole, but sought to favour certain cliques of iniquities, and to make laws to protect them in evil manufactures, and for traffic in tobacco and alcohol.

And no man more sought to be a governor or lawmaker for the good of the people, or to serve Me;

But he sought office for profit's sake and vainglory.

Now, therefore, My holy angels went away from them and no more answered their prayers.

And the righteousness of the first days departed away from them.

And they became a nation of money-getters and servants of mammon.

And I blessed not their marriages nor their households.

And their sons and daughters respected not their fathers and mothers; for, as the fathers and mothers respected not Me, so came disrespect and misery upon them.

And their sons and daughters became profligates and idlers, growing up for no good under the sun, depending on their wits to work out a life of luxury and sin.

And whoso married, peace came not to them; but contention and jealousy and bitterness of heart.

And their offspring fell in grade, becoming outcasts and paupers and criminals.

And husbands and wives cried out for divorcement on all hands.

And the lawmakers granted them and favoured them; but, lo and behold, the evil multiplied on the earth.

In pity I cried out to them, saying: Ye may make laws forever, but My kingdom cometh not by the road of man's laws. Except ye turn about, and begin anew, there is no help for you under the sun.

But they would not hear Me.

Many men shall rise up, saying: If the government would make a law of peace; or, if the government would prohibit the traffic and the manufacture of this curse or that curse,—

But we say unto you, all these things shall fail.

Trust not in the ungodly to do a godlike thing.

The societies shall fail; the Peace Society shall become a farce; the Prohibition Society shall be lost sight of.

Even the churches that shall profess peace and temperance will not embrace peace and temperance. They will fraternize with liquor-traffickers and with colonels and generals of war, for sake of policy.

The boast of the worldly shall be: This is the home for all peoples; but, nevertheless, even in the midst of their boastings they shall make prohibitory laws to the contrary.

For they are fallen under the lower light; none can turn them about the other way.

Under the name of liberty, they shall claim the right to practice ungodliness.

Are these predictions, made in the year 1881, true? Look about you, read the signs of the times.

The Church of Russia has been destroyed. This country is the shadow of things to come throughout the world, not alone in religion, but in government and economy. A shadow is not the reality, but a semblance of it. The destruction of the church introduced a wave of atheism, for the pendulum always swings from one extreme to the other before coming to rest in the median. The new religion of the perfected U. S. S. R. will be worship of the Creator.

The communism of the U. S. S. R. is also but a weak semblance of that which is to come, just as the loose confederacy of the original thirteen states was but a shadow of our present mighty nation. *True* communism is synonymous with *peace* and *democracy*. The U. S. S. R. is but blazing the cooperative trail for the rest of the world, just as the U. S. A. blazed a republican trail afterwards followed by many nations. The U. S. A. and the U. S. S. R. forecast the birth of the United States of the World.

The U. S. S. R. has cut a pattern that will be followed by every major nation. Destruction of privately controlled banking systems is the prerequisite step to the building of a new and better order of life.

The House of Have, rulers of the world through their international banking and capitalistic system, know this. Before the year 1948 the capitalistic countries will gang up on the U. S. S. R. and attempt to destroy her. They have as little love for a cooperative commonwealth, even though it be but the shadow, as King

George the Third had for the little group of states that were the shadow of the coming republic, destined to be the richest, strongest nation the world had seen.

In attempting to destroy the new system of government, the House of Have will destroy itself. The present war will increase in intensity until all nations, either directly or indirectly, are involved. Fascist dictators now control several nations. Since the declaration of war in September, 1939, both England and France have adopted what is equivalent to a dictatorship. This epidemic of dictators will spread until our own nation falls in line and we, too, are Fascist ruled and dictator governed.

Fascist dictators of today are also shadows of things to come. The Fascist dictator of today, placed in power by the House of Have, will be followed by the democratic dictator of tomorrow elected to office by the people. Democratic dictators will be given power because of their ability to lead their countries into peace and plenty, not for their ability to lead in war.

The rule of wealth is in its last days. Not long will war overrun the earth, for in these days of scientific destruction those who live by the instruments of death will die by their own weapons of destruction.

Nine thousand years ago Zarathustra was born in Persia, and was destined to free man from the bondage of the landowners of his day. Six thousand years ago Abraham restored freedom to the people of his time, and three thousand years ago Moses freed the Children of Israel by leading them out of bondage into the new land of promise. The time is near when thousands of our citizens will go forth out of a crumbling civilization to found a renewed order of life in production-for-use, the practice of the Golden Rule, and cooperatives.

God will protect those who acknowledge Him in this cycle as He did in all past cycles.

The manuscripts of the Essenes give the road map for such an exodus, and the blueprint for the erection of a home where peace and plenty may be enjoyed by all who are awake to welcome the dawn of a New Day.

CHAPTER XI

Prophecies of Earthquakes and Continental Changes

Earthquakes and Continental Changes

The destruction of New York City has been prophesied many times by different seers. There seems to be general agreement that the city will first be visited by an earthquake that will tumble the skyscrapers, and afterward the city will sink into the sea. It is quite possible that the light earthquakes which have visited the east and west coasts in the past few months are a warning before the final catastrophe.

At the time of the first world war there lived in Monaco a Jean Buvais, called the sage of Notre Dame de Laguet. This man had great power over the peasants of this principality, as he was credited with being ninety per cent accurate in his prophecies covering a period of forty years. Buvais called a forty-day prayer meeting of the peasants, so that by the power of prayer the lost continent of Atlantis should be prevented from rising from its ocean bed, which would have caused the wickedest sections of the world to disappear.

Several scientists concur with the auguries of the seers. William Boeksche, a German scientist, has predicted great changes in the earth's surface, and climatic changes affecting the whole world. In an address at Halle he prophesied tremendous geological submersions to which recent strange weather vagaries, storms, floods, earthquakes, and volcanic action are the prelude. Herr Boeksche thinks that these changes may come with relative suddenness and that we are on the eve of great terrestial convulsions. New continents and mountain ranges may be expected to rise out of the Pacific.

Dr. Milton A. Nobles, geologist and student of earthquakes and volcanic phenomena, predicts a second deluge during which whole continents will be wiped out and new ones created. He sees new lands rising to double the area of the Western Hemisphere, and states that Australia and New Zealand will join in a continent three times their present size. He prophesies the shortening of the earth's axis, with a new North Pole in Siberia and a new South Pole in the South Pacific Ocean. There will be, he states, a new equator, with the United States so close that the all-year mildness of Florida will be the whole nation's temperature. New sea coasts in the Atlantic and Pacific will arise, making Los Angeles, San Francisco, and other ports, inland cities. The Gulf of Mexico will be transformed into an inland sea the size of Texas, and Central America and the West Indies amalgamated in the new America, 5,000 miles wide.

While many of the scientists laughed at Dr. Nobles' theories, the fact remains that earthquakes, volcanic eruptions and tidal waves have occurred in zones indicated by Dr. Nobles.

The prophetic tables of the Essenes tell us that we live in a time of overlapping of several cycles, the most important, so far as earth changes are concerned, being the 24,000-year period.

Mu, or Pan, sank in the Pacific 24,000 years ago.

This catastrophe was the basis of the tales of a flood recorded in the Bible in the allegory of Noah and the Ark, and in the mythology of all races and peoples. Le Plongeon discovered a manuscript centuries old of the Mayas of Yucatan entitled, "The Torano Manuscript," which is now in the British Museum. The manuscript was translated by Le Plongeon:

In the year 6 Kan, on the 11th Mulac in the month of Zac, there occurred terrible earthquakes which continued without interruption until the 13th Chuen. The country of the hills of Pan, the land of Mu, was sacrificed; being twice upheaved it suddenly disappeared during the night, the basin being continually shaken by volcanic forces. Being confined, these caused the land to sink and to rise several times and in various places. At last the surface gave way and ten countries were torn asunder and scattered; unable to stand the force of the convulsions, they sank with their 65,000,000 inhabitants.

Further information pertaining to the sinking of Pan, of which Ja-Pan is the only remnant, may be found in the American Bible, *OAHSPE*.

There is unlimited geologic evidence of tropical foliage unearthed in the Arctic regions, arctic animals uncovered in tropical excavations, sea-shells on mountain tops, etc., indicating that several great temperature and geologic changes have occurred in the past.

What has occurred in the past can happen in the present, so the changes predicted for these days are not at all impossible.

143

CHAPTER XII

Exoteric and Esoteric Astrology

Two distinct systems of astrology have come down to us from ancient philosophers. The one most popular and best known among students of today is the geocentric, wherein the earth is considered as the center of the solar system with the sun and planets moving around it. This system is not astronomically correct, but as we live on the earth and not on the sun, it is believed that the appearances of the sun and planets in their relations to us would provide a means of judging their effects upon material things. The experience of countless astrological students seems to justify this belief. The Essene system is called HELIOCENTRIC because it accepts the true position of the sun as the center and master of the solar system and provides a mode of interpretation that can be verified mathematically and astronomically. Essene astrology, or cosmogony, is confirmed by the mathematics of Einstein, the astronomy of the Mt. Wilson and other observatories, and every event in the history of the race.

Popular astrology is geocentric, and relates to earthly things and the material condition of mankind, therefore is terrestial and exoteric, while the heliocentric system is concerned with the evolutionary principle in nature, and is related to the spiritual and intellectual development of humanity.

144

Every superstition and belief that has been accepted by man over a period of time has within it an element of truth, though the foundation of such superstition may be in error. While exoteric, or geocentric astrology is based upon a false premise, we find evidence of its

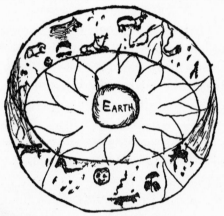

Zodiac of the Ancients. Used by Pyramid Astronomers

truth in the cycle of Uranus, a large, slowly moving planet. Commencing at the birth date of our independence, 1776, a year which marked a beneficent change for the people of our continent, we add to this 84 years—the time it takes Uranus to make her cycle through the signs—and we are at 1860, the Civil War, with its birth of freedom for the slaves. Another cycle of Uranus and another 84 years brings us to 1944, which will prove to be of more importance to the United States than did either of the preceding dates.

Long ago Neptune began her transit through Virgo and brought an invention to the Chinese that proved more valuable in the spread of light than any other before or since, the art of printing. Later, this same condition paralleled the translation and printing of the King James Bible. As far back as we have records we find that wars, revolutions, and social upheavals accompany Neptune through Virgo, and we are apt to consider this aspect as being one of malefic and destructive influences. This interpretation is a most unfortunate error, and is but another proof of the tendency of the human to turn a deaf ear to the voice of infallible wisdom, the Creator, whose "worlds in splendor are the scroll on which His hands write His almighty will and boundless love." Every seeming adverse condition should serve but to develop our powers and exercise the talents with which we are endowed. Such periods generate the force by which we may forge ahead to greater accomplishments.

Today we have before us a period of golden opportunity, enabling us to have full emancipation from the limitations of the past. Many will turn their talents into destructive channels and succumb, while others will forge ahead into a new and better age.

The years until 1944 will witness most revolutionary changes. Not only upon the strength of astrological configuration do we say this, but because of the fact that at this time of world destiny, there is a convergence of several cycles of time which, coming to a common point simultaneously, carry a tremendous portent.

Transcendent over all is the overlapping of the 24,000-year cycle in the development of man and the processional cycle of 25,826.5 years. This convergence of the two major cycles marks a period of continental cataclysms similar to that which existed at the time of the sinking of the continent of Mu (Lemuria or Pan). This continent extended from the northeastern coast of Australia to Ja-Pan, (a remnant of Pan) and was submerged in the Arc of Noe. During the coming continental changes, the submerged continent of Pan will rise out of the waters of the Pacific.

The Essene system of astrology (or cosmogony) has been esoteric throughout the ages. Popular astrological literature is only concerned with the geocentric system, which meets the needs of the people for a superficial and material form of the science. The Essene heliocentric system is only understood by a few adepts and is a secret

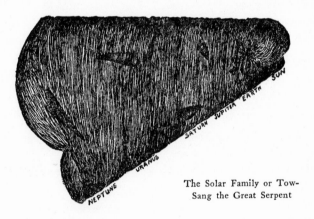

The Solar Family or Tow-
Sang the Great Serpent

branch of knowledge. Herein the cardinal features only are given, for an understanding of the unseen and its relation to the seen is an essential for further progress into the science of prophecy.

The true science of astrological cosmogony consists of a knowledge of the cyclic revolutions in nature on both the physical and super-physical planes. The research work and compilation of statistics now being accomplished by several astrological organizations, both here and in Europe, will fail to uncover the "lost secrets" of cosmological astrology, for the basis of their investigations is fallacious.

A true understanding of prophecy (and astrology is one phase of prophecy) can only come with an understanding of the CREATOR'S CLOCK and its use in discovering the dates of changes in human affairs. These changes are governed by the changing environment of the earth as it travels with other members of the solar family through interplanetary space. This space is not a vacuum, but is filled with corporeal substance of differing rates of vibration and degrees of density.

Four
The Number of the Earth

The earth's number is four, symbolized by the rectangle. Mother Earth and all her offspring are governed by this number. All go through four stages in the cycle from the unseen into the seen and back again into the unseen.

The Cosmic Cause of War

Astronomical Name	Essene Name	Motion or Vibration	Manifestation	Relative Density	Aspect
Ether	Ethe	100	Life & health	1	Light
Cosmic dust	A'ji	66	War-revolution	4	Semi-light
Nebula	Ji'ay	33	Epidemics-fevers	16	Semi-dark
Planet earth	Corpor	0	Death	256	Dark

Whenever there is a precipitation of a'ji or cosmic dust upon the earth it causes mankind to become aggressive and war upon his neighbors. In 1914, the precipitation of a'ji increased both in Europe and the Orient

148

and a heavy rain of this cosmic dust will continue to fall until the year 1944. As the fall of a'ji eases off, the fall of ji'ay will continue, following up an epidemic of wars with an epidemic of disease and pestilence. Beginning with the year 1948, ji'ay will in turn gradually cease to fall, and the earth will enter a brilliant area in interplanetary space less contaminated with corporeal dust. As we enter this region of light, there will be great spiritual manifestations upon earth. This new condition has been interpreted by Christian peoples as the "second coming of Christ."

Thothma, Pharaoh of Egypt, Builder of the Great Pyramid

The travel of the solar family can be timed upon the Creator's clock and future events foretold with mathematical accuracy by one possessed of spiritual insight. This clock may be used for every cycle or series of cycles, for it pertains to all creation. In the words of Thothma, builder of the great pyramid of Gizeh, "As a diameter is to a circle, and a circle is to a diameter, so are the rules of the seasons of the earth."

History is always written according to the bias and nationality of the historian. Recent history contains much error; over a thousand years in the past history is quite unreliable; beyond six thousand years practically nothing is known. It is only when we turn to the manuscripts of the Essenes that we can find a history of the ancient past confirmed by every contemporaneous discovery and research of archeology.

Every world event bears witness that we are at the end of a major cycle in the evolution of man. Taking past history as a guide, it is evident that at this time there will be complete changes in world affairs, and the several world religions and empires will pass away with the birth of a new civilization.

Nature on all her planes, seen and unseen, unfolds her possibilities in a series of successive world cycles. As the earth is subject to a cycle of seasons—spring, summer, autumn, and winter—so is the sun with its family of planets obedient to a great cycle of about 24,000 years. During this time it travels a major arc of its orbit. This 24,000 year cycle should not be confused with the 26,000 year cycle of travel around a smaller orbit, nor should it be confused with the local polar-motion cycle of the earth, which completes its period in about 25,700 years.

The fact is well known that the earth has at least five different motions. Each of these motions has its own orbit and cycle, and each cycle has its influence on human unfoldment. To explain each cycle, and its effect, would require a textbook on cosmogony and would be beyond the depth of the average person, hence only the essentials of esoteric astrology will be given. A profound knowledge of the cycles would disclose all the important epochs of mankind's evolution, the geologic ages, and changes in topography and temperature of the earth.

The periods of human progress and retrogression, the light and dark eras, the rise and fall of empires, the times of enlightenment and ignorance, the seasons of peace and plenty, of wars and revolutions, and of every other major world event will be found to obey the law of cyclic periodicity.

What concerns us now, however, is the demonstrable fact that the world is passing through the first hundred year phase of the current 3,000 year cycle known as Kosmon,* when all institutions that have held sway during the past 3,000 year cycle will be disintegrated to permit the development of a new and better order.

The earth's number was recognized by the ancients as being four. As there are four seasons on the earth, so also are there four steps in the cycle of manifestation of everything upon earth. By the ancients the four seasons of manifestation were termed semu, hotu, adu, and uz, corresponding to birth, maturity, senility, and death. Uz was considered the fourth dimension of matter and is the principle of disintegration, whose function it is to dissolve back to the elemental state all things which the principle of life can no longer use. The present chaotic state of world society is called uz because it is given over to uz to be destroyed as former civilizations were destroyed to make way for our present civilization. This process was spoken of by John and Jesus as the fall of Babylon.

The years between 1848 and 1948 make up a 99-year intermediate sub-cycle of the master Kosmon cycle. In this century both uz, marking the death of our civi-

* Kosmon is equivalent to the Aquarian Age. It is the term applied to that section of interplanetary space entered by our planet Earth in 1848 and through which it will travel for three thousand years. It is also the period in the evolution of mankind when a condition of balance of physical and spiritual faculties will be attained. It is the period of maturity for race man, just as the age from 21 to 28 years brings maturity to individual man. Kosmon will bring forth a new race, a new universal religion, a new civilization and a new system of economy.

lization, and semu, witnessing the birth of a new order, occupy the world stage.

Uz of the old cycle is about to make his exit, while semu of the new has just made her entrance. During the few years left for uz to play his part, he will be a

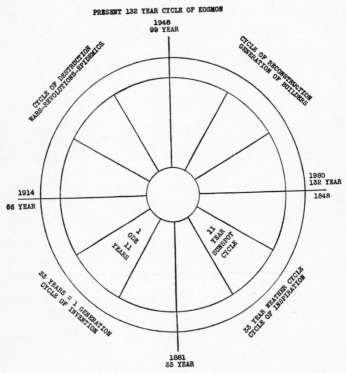

The Creator's Clock Showing the First 132 Year Cycle of Kosmon

busy entity, for he will cause the vanishment of usury and capitalism with its private profit system based on the ownership of land. With the passing of uz, the present system, whereby a man can own land that he is not personally using, will go out.

152

Semu brings with her a new order of things and the establishment of a better and more progressive state for the whole human race. Mankind is fast emerging from the bondage of the past. The old despotic systems of feudalism and superstitions fostered by the House of Have, both in the East and West, are fast being liquidated by modern research, discovery, and invention. There is a tremendous speeding-up process in evidence. Unseen spiritual forces are pressing on the psychic side of all humanity and causing a stimulation of intellectual and spiritual potentialities. Individuals and races everywhere are demanding their primary rights. Nations and classes, still bound by old traditions and customs of the dark ages, are now subject to great upheavals.

Democratic institutions based on the principle of freedom are everywhere gaining increased approval in the hearts of mankind. The reactionary trend of the old order in evidence in many countries is destined to defeat. The discoveries and science of Kosmon are levelling all divisions and barriers among the peoples of the earth, and will bring into existence a new consciousness of the unity and solidarity of the human race. There are to be equal rights for all classes and nations in every part of the globe.

The great democracies of free people which respect the rights of the individual are enlightened and progressive. Nations that are not free, where the individual is submerged, are backward and unawakened. Their state is one of spiritual darkness and lethargy. The path of progress for them is the hard path of revolution and chaos. Where force rules, reason is dethroned and individual freedom is suppressed. Force is always met by a greater force, therefore causes are set up leading to terrible reaction. Not only is there plenty of evidence of this in history, but every great religious literature testifies to its truth.

Democratic countries have had a spirit of tolerance and good will, a willingness to negotiate with all other peoples, so that a peaceful solution could be found without resort to force. The primary rights of man are recognized as the basic factor to the foundation of a new world order of international peace and security.

CHAPTER XIII

Origin and Destiny of Man

There is a grand cosmic day of one hundred and forty-four thousand years, just as the minor earth day is one of twenty-four hours. The Book of Revelation speaks of 144,000 being saved, and Bible students have interpreted this as meaning 144,000 persons. 144,000 years pertains to the period of time man exists on earth, for race-man is born (se'mu), attains maturity (ho'tu), passes into senility (a'du), and death (uz), in 144,000 years. Man was first born upon earth about 72,000 years ago. At that time, the earth was in darkness with a prevailing temperature of approximately 98 degrees, or blood heat. In 72,000 years the earth will have become so cold that it will no longer be habitable, and man will have ceased to propagate. The year 1848 marked the halfway point of man's habitation of the earth. During the present, or Kosmon, cycle the sixth race will be born with spiritual and physical senses equally developed. The new race will recognize things of the spirit equally as well as those of the flesh.

This is all covered in the Bible, but few have the understanding to interpret the myths and allegories concealing these truths. The Bible, from cover to cover, is an allegory of the four stages of man upon earth. It is a mistake to accept the Bible literally. There is no basis, in fact, for the belief that individual man can spiritualize the body to the point where it is immortal. But race-man will, in another 72,000 years, have attained to such a degree of spirituality that the physical will have been entirely conquered and man will have become godlike.

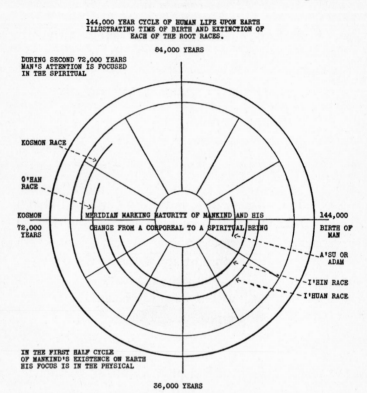

144,000 YEAR CYCLE OF HUMAN LIFE UPON EARTH ILLUSTRATING TIME OF BIRTH AND EXTINCTION OF EACH OF THE ROOT RACES.

84,000 YEARS

DURING SECOND 72,000 YEARS MAN'S ATTENTION IS FOCUSED IN THE SPIRITUAL

KOSMON RACE

O'HAN RACE

KOSMON
72,000 YEARS

MERIDIAN MARKING MATURITY OF MANKIND AND HIS CHANGE FROM A CORPOREAL TO A SPIRITUAL BEING

144,000

BIRTH OF MAN

A'SU OR ADAM

I'HIN RACE

I'HUAN RACE

IN THE FIRST HALF CYCLE OF MANKIND'S EXISTENCE ON EARTH HIS FOCUS IS IN THE PHYSICAL

36,000 YEARS

The Book of Genesis tells of man's birth on earth as Adam or animal man. Adam corresponds to the first sub-human race a'su, born upon earth 78,000 years ago. This race was animal, did not have self or I AM consciousness and was not immortal. Only by the crossing of the angels (spirit) with a'su (animal) was man, possessing both body and soul, given birth. Then self

156

(soul) or I AM consciousness came into existence and not before.

In Genesis, we have the beginning of time; in Revelation, we have the end of time. In Genesis, we have the first heaven and the first earth; in Revelation, we see a new heaven and a new earth where God is All in All. The self has then become the Not-self, or Super-self, the soul merged in the Over-soul and Nirvana attained.

Progression is the major rule of the universe. Mineral, vegetable, animal, and man are the four visible

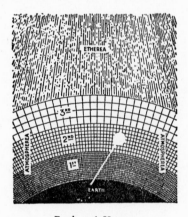

Earth and Heavens

life planes. There are three major life planes in the unseen which complete the sacred seven.

The relationship existing between the seven planes is shown in the following chart.

THE SEVEN PLANES OF BEING

Seven Planes of Being and Seven Steps in Unfoldment

Three Dimensional World of Matter

FOUR LIFE PLANES IN THE VISIBLE OR SEEN

MANKIND. Self-conscious,
Physical, mental and spiritual bodies concentric.
Soul in embryo, beginning of soul unfoldment.
Powers of reason, locomotion on, above and under
the earth. Procreation and growth.

ANIMAL KINGDOM. Physical and spiritual
bodies manifest, mental body in embryo. Soul
conceived.
Simple consciousness of existence and environment.
Existence for a season only after death in the
lowest heaven adjacent to the earth.
Power of locomotion, procreation, growth, and
elemental thought.

VEGETABLE KINGDOM. Physical body only.
Elementary consciousness like that of deep sleep.
Spiritual body in embryo.
Ability to change mineral molecules into vegetable
cells.
Reacts to heat, gravity, pressure, and light.

MINERAL KINGDOM. Physical embodiment
only. Embryonic consciousness like that of deep
trance.
Power of elements to react to affinities and combine
with other elements to form a compound.

Read up.

158

ETHEREAN HEAVENS or Etherea located in interstellar space.

Plane of Cosmic Consciousness.

Power to travel anywhere in creation.

The Third Resurrection.

Spiritual and intellectual grades of 100 and above.

THE BRIDGE OF CHINVAT

ORGANIC HEAVENS or SECOND RESURRECTION located thousands of miles from the earth's surface but within the atmosphere of the earth and in the earth's vortex.

Plane of Universal Consciousness. Soul in expression.

The Self submerged in the Not-Self, Nirvana.

The throne of God, Chief Executive of the Red Star Earth.

Power to assist lower grades in spiritual progression.

Ability to travel anywhere within the atmospherean boundaries of the earth.

INORGANIC HEAVENS or FIRST RESURRECTION located on and adjacent to the earth's surface. Purgatory wherein souls are purged of selfishness.

The Plane of Super-Consciousness.

Spiritual and mental bodies manifest, physical body discarded. Soul unfolding.

Self is still the major consideration.

Power to travel in the lower heavens only. Travel as instantaneous as thought.

Ability to influence lower grades either for progression or retrogression.

Read up.

THREE GRADES OF SPIRITUAL AND SOUL PROGRESSION IN THE UNSEEN.

159

The races of man are shown on the drawings. We, of this generation, are of the Ghan race. The Kosmon Cycle will give birth to the Kosmon race. A few of the children on earth at this time are of this new sixth race. The Kosmon race will result from the mating of those members of the Ghan race who are the most advanced in spirituality and intelligence. This selection is now being accomplished by unseen forces, and will result in an inspired genetics.

ORIGIN OF MAN

A'su (Adam) appeared upon earth about 78,000 years before the Kosmon Era, and survived eight thousand

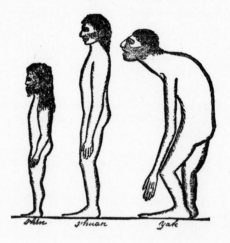

years before becoming extinct. A'su lived upon earth for six thousand years before the appearance of I'hins, who were a cross between materialized angels and A'su.

Approximately a thousand years after the appearance of the I'hin race, this race bred with the A'su again, and the cross between the I'hins and A'su resulted in the birth of a new race called the Druk. The Druks came in about 71,000 years ago.

Within a thousand years following the birth of the Druks, another race resulted from crossing the Druks and A'su. The new race was the Yaks, a race so low in grade as not to be capable of speech, or any inspiration as to eternal life. They were made eunuchs by the I'hins and used as servants.

About 70,000 years B.K. (before Kosmon, or prior to 1848), the Druks and I'hins co-mingled, the result being the *I'huan* race. American Indians are remnants of this race.

About 14,000 years ago, the crossing of the I'hin and I'huan races resulted in the *Ghan* race, to which the Caucasian race belongs.

The I'hins as a race became extinct upon the earth about 3,000 years B.K. Mummies of both I'hins and I'huans have been found in Mexico. The I'hins were small, blond people, while the I'huans were quite large, many being over seven feet tall. The Moundbuilders of Ohio were I'hins.

Cosmic dust (a'ji) will cease to fall in 1947–8, and the earth will pass into the light of the Kosmon era. The Kosmon race will then begin to appear, the result of the amalgamation on the American continent of all the races.

The negroid and oriental races are remnants of the Druks; the Latins are mongrel races between the Druks and I'huan.

The races in the order of their birth upon earth are as follows: 1. A'su; 2. I'hin; 3. Druk; 4. Yak; 5. I'huan; 6. Ghan; 7. Kosmon.

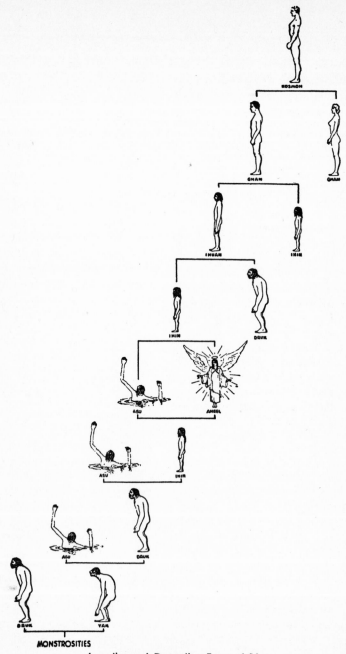

MONSTROSITIES

Ascending and Descending Races of Man

162

The Bible

And the Lord God caused a deep sleep to fall upon Adam, and he slept: and he took one of his ribs, and closed up the flesh thereof.

And the rib which the Lord God had taken from man, made he woman, and brought her unto the man.

And Adam said, "This is now bone of my bones, and flesh of my flesh; she shall be called Woman because she was taken out of man.
—Genesis 2:21–23

The sons of God saw the daughters of man that they were fair; and they took wives of all which they chose.

There were giants in the earth in those days; and also after that, when the sons of God came in unto the daughters of men, and they bare children to them, the same became mighty men.
—Genesis 6:2–4

There is no record existing of any spiritist phenomena of a physical nature in modern times prior to March 31st, 1848, marking the birth of the Kosmon Era.

During the first 33-year cycle, from 1848 to 1881, there were many good materializing mediums. Now there are few.

In a materialization, the ectoplasmic substance, used by a disembodied spirit to form the semblance of their former corporeal body, is drawn through the side of the medium.

It is probable that some similar process of materialization was used by the angels to produce bodies in which to function for the short time required to mate with the A'suans that man might be born.

A'su was an animal devoid of self-consciousness. The angels were spiritual beings. The cross resulted in the birth of the I'hins or little, blond, holy people who possessed animal and spiritual capacities in equal degree. The I'hins could cognize spirits equally as well as mortals. Therefore it was not essential that the angels retain their corporeal forms in order to instruct, guide and guard the I'hins. The I'hins were comparable to a baby for they represented the infant stage of the human race.

In Kosmon man attains that stage of development comparable to that of the adult of twenty-one years of age. Kosmon represents the meridian of spiritual and corporeal development as well as the period of time man inhabits the earth.

Science has long sought the "missing link" or the bridge between ape and man. This link will never be found for the bodies used by angels in their temporary

163

manifestation in corporeal form disintegrated immediately at the end of the angel's need for a corporeal body.

The Kosmon Revelations
In the Archives of the Essenes

Man I made out of the combined elements of every living thing that preceded him, and with the characteristics of all of them. Man was without understanding, unconscious of his creation; not knowing whence he came, nor knowing his own species. Man was void of speech, and more dumb and helpless than any other living creature, and incapable of immortality; and I called him A'su.

Near the end of the se'muan age I took Earth out of the dark regions, and brought her into the light of My etherean worlds, where dwelt countless millions of spirits of the dead who had died in infancy on other corporeal worlds. To these angels I said:

"Behold, a new world have I created like unto the places ye were quickened into life. Come ye and enjoy it, and ye shall learn from it how it was with other worlds in ages past."

And there came to the new earth millions of angels from etheria. And now was earth in the latter days of se'mu, and the angels could readily take on corporeal bodies. Out of se'muan elements clothed they themselves with flesh and bones, and took on corporeal forms.

And these angels, having died in infancy, comprehended not procreation, nor corporeal life; and they dwelt with the Asuans and brought forth a new race, called I'hin, capable of immortality.

Then I took Earth out of se'mu, and the angels gave up their corporeal bodies. To them I said,

"Because ye brought forth such as shall be your joint heirs in heaven, ye shall tread the earth with your feet, and walk by the side of the newly born, being guardian angels over them, for they are your own flesh and kin.

"Fruit of your seed have I quickened with my spirit, and man shall come forth with a birthright to My etherean worlds. As I have quickened the seed of the first born, so will I quicken all seed to the end of Earth. And each and every man-child and woman-child born into life, will I quicken with a new spirit, which shall proceed out of Me at the time of conception. Neither will I give to any spirit of the higher or lower heavens power to enter a womb, or the fetus of a womb, and be born again.

"As the corporeal Earth passes away, so shall pass away the first race A'su. But as I pass not away, so shall not pass away the spirit of man."

Physical and Spiritual Balance of the Races According to Mendel's Principles of Heredity

A'SU			ANGEL		
100% physical (animal man)			100% spiritual (spiritual woman)		
DESCENDING ORDER			*ASCENDING ORDER*		
	Physical	*Spiritual*		*Physical*	*Spiritual*
A'SU	16/16	0	I'HIN	8/16	8/16
DRUK	12/16	4/16	IHUAN	10/16	6/16
YAK	14/16	2/16	GHAN	9/16	7/16
MONSTROS-ITIES	15/16	1/16	KOSMON	8/16	8/16

Individual Man Is a Recapitulation of Racial Development

Race Man	*Individual Man*		*Consciousness*
I'HIN	INFANT	Age 0–7	SELF
IHUAN	CHILD	7–14	FAMILY
GHAN	YOUTH	14–21	NATIONAL
KOSMON	MANHOOD	21–28	WORLD

There have been five races. A'su or Adam was a subhuman, more animal than man, and did not have self-consciousness. A'su can not correctly be termed a race of man.

The Druks and Yaks were of a descending order; the Ihin, Ihuan, and Ghan races of an ascending order. We are of the Ghan or fifth race. Kosmon marks the meridian of racial unfoldment and this race will possess an equal development of both the physical and spiritual attributes. From now on, man's attention will be focused in the spiritual realms more than the physical. Spiritual concepts will come into the ascendency, while physical ones will decline. Kosmon will give birth to the sixth race.

It is readily observed that a correspondence exists between race man and individual man in the development of the faculties. Individual man is the miniature of race-man, and in his unfoldment from infancy to maturity is a recapitulation of the unfoldment of the race.

The first race upon earth was the I'hin, and in this race a balance existed between the physical and the spiritual. This race had psychic faculties equal to its physical senses, and could cognize the angels as well as

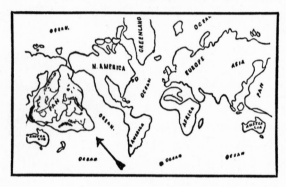

Map of the Submerged Continent in the
Pacific Ocean. (Pan or Mu)

Drawn in 1881 by John B. Newbrough. In 1933 the existence of Pan or Mu was verified from soundings made in the Pacific by the officers of the Ramapo, a U. S. Geodetic Survey vessel.

man, but being an infant race, it was like a child whose intellect is potential only.

It has taken 72,000 years for man to develop a brain and learn to use reasoning faculties. It seems, as one looks around the world today, that some of us haven't yet learned to use our brains any too well.

As the Kosmon race matures it will re-establish a balance between the physical and the spiritual. It will be like the I'hins, with the addition that the intellect, judgment, reason, and discrimination will also be un-

166

folded. With the development of both intellect and spirituality, the self gives way to the Not-self, or Super-self. Consciousness progresses to the realization that the wisest selfishness is unselfishness; competition gives way to co-operation, and a United States of the World replaces rabid nationalism.

As the races of mankind evolve, they gradually progress from a consciousness of self to that of family, tribal, city, and national consciousness. The present world war will purge the race of the belief that any nation or race is superior, and bring the realization that we are all members of one great human family born to live our brief span on Mother Earth and *share* her bounties so that all may prosper in peace and plenty.

The life span of race-man upon earth is shown on the 144,000 year cosmic clock. Each of the twelve divisions of the clock represents a 12,000 year cycle. You will note that the point on this cosmic clock corresponding to 12 on our physical clocks is in the *east*, rather than at the top, or north. This is because our planet revolves from east to west. As the sun rises in the east and sets in the west, likewise did civilization begin in the east and will reach its zenith in the west. In the year 1848 gold was discovered in California and migration started westward, leading to the settlement of the entire continent from the eastern to the western coast and indirectly to the opening up of Japan to the western nations.

When Japan lowered her barriers, travel and communication became common with all nations. This in turn enabled the dragon or money power, with its usury, capitalism, commercialism, imperialism, and its exploitation of backward peoples, to plant the seeds of the first and second world wars.

Mankind is focused in a three-dimensional physical environment. As long as he resides in a physical body

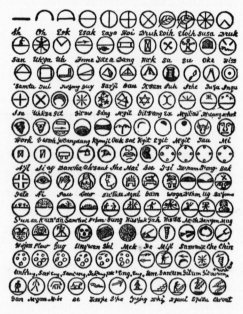

Panic or First Written Language Developed by Man.
Used on Pan or Mu

there is action and reaction between the physical and the spiritual man. One side can not be injured or developed without its effect on the other. There is also a relationship between the spirit, intellect, and sex consciousness.

DEGREES IN EVOLUTION AS EVIDENCED BY SEX CONSCIOUSNESS

MOTTO: The higher the altitude attained, the deeper the possible fall.

1. THE ANIMAL—"Perfect in its order." Has no sex consciousness operating outside its own species or order.

2. A'SU—High enough to have this consciousness, but not high enough to discriminate; hence he "knew not his own species."
3. I'HIN—Appears to have received this consciousness in what may be called the discriminative degree.
4. DRUK—Divided into two classes:
   A. Those who could be taught this discrimination.
   B. Those incapable of being so taught.
5. YAK—Incapable of being so taught.
6. I'HUAN—Appears to have been of similar sex-consciousness as the I'hins, but nearer the earth, as shown by a more powerful physique and earthly desires.

The possibilities of progress or degree of potentiality of spirit are largely indicated through sex manifestations.

Man is a link in a mighty chain of correspondences reaching back to primordial dust. He does not seem to be significant or explainable save as a part of this long chain which links him to the past. Furthermore, if man is anything, he must be the culmination, or focusing point, of all that was or is in the long sequence of events that led up to his present state. His roots go all the way back to cosmic "blueprints." He is inseparably linked to all the past and to all the future. There never was any "fall" of man. Man is ever ascending. The cosmogony in the Book of Genesis belongs to the Mother Goose childish fables of the race.

Mankind is the product of eugenics governed and directed by the Over-Ruling Intelligence of all creation. The Essenes know Him as Jehovah. We are now at the halfway mark in race unfoldment. Seventy-two thousand years hence the man of that day will be as superior to the man of today as man is superior to a chimpanzee.

CHAPTER XIV

THE CREATOR'S CLOCK AND THE LAWS OF PERIODICITY

Science is now accepting the fact that there is a distinct periodicity in human affairs in correspondence with various cosmic cycles. Roy Chapman Andrews in his research in ancient civilizations in Mongolia, has discovered, as have other archeologists in various parts of the world, that the rise and fall of civilizations seems to occur over a three thousand-year period.

The builders of the Great Pyramid of Gizeh knew far more of cosmic cycles and their effects than is known by our present-day scientists. Some of the cycles used by the prophets of the Pyramid are herein given. They have been taken from the manuscripts of the Essenes.

In 1908 Dr. George E. Hale of Mt. Wilson Observatory discovered a sun spot cycle of eleven years and a magnetic cycle of twenty-two years. Dr. Charles G. Abbot of Smithsonian Institute has confirmed both the eleven and the twenty-two-year cycle. Dr. Harlan True Stetson of Massachusetts Institute of Technology recently published a book entitled "Sun Spots and Their Effects," containing a summary of what is known pertaining to these cycles.

It is now claimed by various scientists that sun spots affect our weather, increase magnetic disturbances, interfere with radio communications, influence crops, control the amount of ultra-violet rays reaching the earth, govern the visitation of insect pests, and determine fluctuations of business conditions.

Recent research confirms the conclusions of the ancients. Human affairs may be plotted with an astonishing degree of accuracy by one acquainted with cosmic cycles and their meanings.

The prophetic tables of the Essenes are read in a clockwise direction, with 12 in the east instead of the north, as it is on our clock faces. The four quarters of the earth are represented on the Creator's clock with east to the right instead of the left, as on popular astrological charts.

The circle and cross, when divided into twelve equal arcs, represent the timepiece upon which future events may be read in correct relationship with time. This circle and cross are useless without a known date which may be used as a constant. Until revealed in the Essene manuscripts, there had been no known constant which could be used in prophecy. Most interpreters have used the date 1 A.D., the supposed date of Christ's birth, as the point in time from which to work. Biblical and archeological research have brought to light the fact that 1 A.D. is not correct by at least four years, and possibly the error is much greater.

The year 1848 is the date when the earth, in its travel through interplanetary space, entered a new cosmic cycle. *It is a date which may be used with mathematical certainty in the interpretation of prophecy.*

March 31, 1848, gave birth to a new 3,000-year cycle, sometimes called the Aquarian Age. *The first 132 year cycle of Kosmon, or the Aquarian Age, will witness the end of a 72,000, a 36,000, a 24,000, and a 12,000-year cosmic cycle.*

The years 1940 to 1948 are the last seven years of the third quarter of the first 132-year cycle of Kosmon. The 132 years between 1848 and 1980 will see a complete change in every phase of human activity. This period will completely alter the map of the world. New continents will rise, sections of old continents will sink beneath the seas. Our civilization will be destroyed in order to clear the ground for a new civilization superior to any that has preceded it.

The imagination is as unable to visualize the peace, abundance and beauty of life in the world of tomorrow as would the serf of the days of feudalism have been unequal to the foreseeing of the airplane, auto, radio, and other inventions of our day.

Cosmic cycles may be divided into twelve lesser periods of eleven years each corresponding to the recently discovered weather cycle. Three eleven-year cycles make up a quarter of 33 years, corresponding to a generation of man. A 144,000-year cycle is made up of four quarters of 36,000 years or twelve periods of 12,000 years each.

In the 132-year cycle each quarter marks the birth of a new generation of man; in the 144,000-year cycle each hour of 12,000 years marks the birth of a new root race.

The year 1848 A.D., or Kosmon 1, is the key to prophecy. Kosmon 1 or 1 A.K. (1848) marks the year when the spiritual and animal phases of man's character shall begin to equalize. The year 1 A.K. also marks the year of discovery of gold in California, an event which led to the opening up of the West and the building of

172

transcontinental railroads. By making the shipment of agricultural products possible, the railroads were instrumental in the settlement of the western states and the growth in power of this nation.

It was about 1848 that Japan was opened to commerce with the Occidentals. This was an outstanding event in the history of mankind, for it is bearing fruit in the present attempt to dominate the east. The development of imperialistic policies—a lesson learned only too well from the Christian nations—will cause the spread of communism in China and a revolution in Japan. In the latter country we shall see a replacement of the present form of government, which today is a weird conglomeration of Emperor worship, feudalism, and capitalism. It will be replaced by a totalitarian state functioning for the benefit of the people of Japan rather than for the aggrandizement of a small group of families who, now, more completely own the means of production in Japan than do our sixty families here in the United States.

The year 1848 is a key year in the life of our planet. It marks the birth of the Kosmon Era, the Aquarian Age, the millennium of a thousand years of peace, God's kingdom on earth, or whatever term you wish to apply to a condition of peace, plenty, and security. However, the complete manifestation of the millennium, foretold by every major prophet, will not take place until the year 1980.

The eleven-year cycle is the minor cycle of prophecy. It is the sun spot, magnetic, and minor weather cycle. The major weather cycle is the 33-year cycle. There is always a correspondence between the cycles of man and the planet that gave him birth. There are three generations to a hundred years, and 33 marks the time of a generation of man. Therefore, if we add 33 years to 1848, we find 1881, the year the Essene histories were recovered. It is more than a coincidence that the Oneida community started in 1848 as a pure fraternity of peaceful communists living the life and abiding by the teachings of the early Essenes. It lasted just 33 years, and was converted into a capitalistic enterprise in the year 1881.

The year 1881 marks the production of many books and prophecies of an inspirational nature. It was the high noon of a minor cosmic day. The sunset of this 132-year day, the year 1914, sixty-six years after the birth of the Kosmon Era, witnessed the preview of the war of Armageddon.

A period of thirty-three years of warfare on earth began in the year 1914. Before this present cycle of thirty-three years ushers in the next thirty-three-year cycle in 1948, the troubles foretold in the Books of Daniel and Revelation will have come to pass. The years from 1914 to 1948 are a cycle which will see the passing of the capitalistic form of society, will mark the death of imperialism, will witness the downfall of Fascism, and will convert every major nation into a co-operative commonwealth.

The thirty-three-year cycle starting in 1948 will be a cycle of reconstruction for a better and wiser world. By 1980 every prophecy of Edward Bellamy, Henry George, Tolstoy, Newbrough and other farsighted men will have been fulfilled.

The fifty-year cycle is one pertaining to manifestations in the heavens of the earth. In the early days of our planet, the graduation of immortals from the highest heavens of the earth into the Etherian Heavens took place only every 200 years. Now, this event takes place every 50 years. The year 1980, the termination of four 50-year cycles, will be a grand time in the heavens, for it will see the graduation of the largest host in the history of the Red Star, Earth.

The one-thousand-year cycle is recognized in the Bible, for it is said that God's day is as a thousand years. Three thousand years mark the time of the rise and fall of a civilization. Every three thousand years the religions of the world change, for it is harvest time in the heavens. Every three thousand years witnesses conditions similar to those prevailing today—the downfall of religions that have served their purpose in the unfoldment of the talents of man, and the return to world-wide worship of one God only, the Creator.

In the past the All One, Creator, Architect of the Universe, the I AM that I Am, Jehovah, or whatever term you prefer to apply to the source of all, has been known by many names. The American Indians knew Him as Egoquim, the Great Spirit; the ancients knew Him as Ormazd or Light; and Moses knew Him as Jehovah, whose name it was forbidden to mention in the hearing of idol worshippers.

Here it may be well to explain the key to JHVH, the unpronounceable word. JHVH was used in exoteric manuscripts open to the public, and, to the initiated, signified the missing letters, E-O-A. This custom is in use today by Free Masons, for in their manuals letters are deleted, making the instructions meaningless to the uninitiated. In the days of Moses, the name of the

Creator (the I AM THAT I AM), could only be spoken in a whisper, mouth to ear, that it might not come into the possession of the profane. In Masonic rituals, a word is used today as a substitute for the lost word.

Peoples have turned away from the worship of the Architect of the Universe and now worship lesser gods. By 1980, the prevailing religions of today—Christianity, Buddhism, Mohammedanism, and Brahmanism —will have passed. Following the war of Armageddon, unity of worship will again be prevalent upon the earth; and with unity of religion will come unity of government, economics, and freedom for all mankind.

Every religion has its purpose. Good, during the time it commands the respect of the people, after the lessons it was sent to teach have been learned, it must be put away as the child puts away his picture-books when he learns to read. Christianity has served a great purpose. Christian nations have brought a more abundant life to many nations in their development of machine production. While their policies have been imperialistic (selfish) in the exploitation of weaker peoples, it was through this same exploitation that resources were developed which would have been undiscovered and potential were it not for the energies and ambitions of these same Christian nations.

Had Perry never forced Japan to open her ports to world trade, Japan today would be as backward as she was a century ago. Today Japan is applying lessons learned from her Christian neighbors and, in her effort to exploit China as England has India, is forcing China again to take her place as a major nation. China is destined to become a leading world nation—by peace and not by war. She has never forgotten the lessons of Chine and Confucius. She has remembered them far better than Israel (America) and better than the Jews have remembered the instructions of Moses and the Nazarene.

Twelve 1000-year cycles compose one-half of the cosmic day, and as it takes two twelve-hour periods to make one day of twenty-four hours, so does it also take two twelve 1000-year cycles to complete the sidereal day.

The twelve thousand-year cycle is divided into quarters of 3000 years each. Three thousand years ago Moses led the Children of Israel out of Egypt and established a peaceful, non-resistant people who worshipped only the Creator. Six thousand years ago Abraham led the slaves out of a disintegrating civilization and established a new nation. Nine thousand years ago Zarathustra (source of Zoroastrian legends) gave humanity its first Bible and established a nation of peace and plenty.

Today we are in a new three thousand-year cycle. The same old story is being reenacted in China. For nine years communism has been developing in northwest China and for nine years the communists were surrounded by hostile troops. Is it not remarkable that Chiang Kai-shek professes Christianity? A few years ago Chiang Kai-shek was doing his utmost to destroy the Red army; and, in order to avoid destruction, this army made a six thousand mile march—about twice the width of the American Continent—and made it on foot over terrain too rough for wheeled traffic. The time came when Chiang Kai-shek realized that he was playing Japan's game, reversed his policy and turned to the Red army for help. It was with the assistance of the Red, or Eight Route Army, that Chinese guerrilla resistance was organized. It is the type of fighting learned from this army that is defeating Japan.

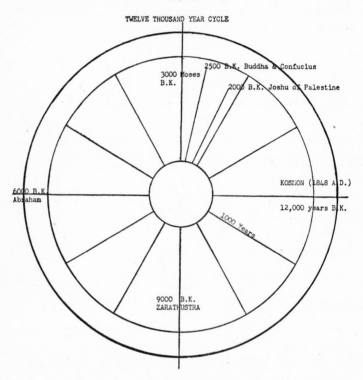

A great lesson may be learned from a study of recent Chinese history. Every great advance in civilization has first been pioneered by a few. These pioneers in thought and action blaze the trail afterwards followed by the thousands. As the Pilgrims first came to America and provided the seed for the United States of today, so did the communists pioneer a new government and economic system that will soon be adopted by all of China. The Reds of China in the Northwest must be credited with a redistribution of the land from the hands of a few large land owners into the hands of thousands of families. The Reds abolished usury, tax-extortion, and eliminated privileged groups. As the Chinese communists taught the unprogressive Chinese a better method of resisting Japanese aggression, so are they also teaching the rest of the nation better government and better economics. They blazed a trail, in their escape from Chiang Kai-shek, that is today being followed by the nation. China is moving her people away from the coast section and taking an entire civilization thousands of miles inland to regions as backward as Japan was a century ago.

Every three thousand years those who are the selected seed of a new civilization are driven out of the nations headed for destruction. As we see the migration of the people from that part of China long controlled by the capitalists of foreign nations, as we see the Jews driven from Germany and establishing a cooperative commonwealth in Palestine, so will we soon see a body of our own citizens, driven by a capitalistic government which will become Fascist, turned out of cities being destroyed by civil war. The year 1944–45 is a crucial year in American history.

Every twenty-four thousand years the earth changes its center of gravity and its axis. The Bible states that when the sign of the Son of Man is in the heavens, these things shall come to pass. Aquarius is the sign of the Son of Man, and the Aquarian Age is equivalent to the

Kosmon Era. It is also said that the moon and stars shall be moved from their places and a new heaven and a new earth shall come to pass. Whenever the earth changes to a new axis, the location of sun and stars are changed from an earthly viewpoint. Then comes a change in climate; the arctic regions become warm; the sea bottom becomes dry land, and mountains are submerged.

In California we have a mine located on top of a

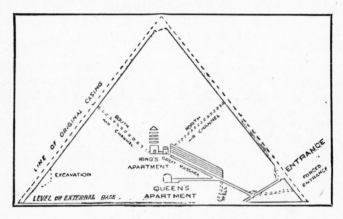

Rooms and Passages of the Great Pyramid

mountain from which oyster shells are dug. It is the change in the earth's axis every twenty-four thousand years that accounts for the former ice-caps in now temperate regions, and explains the finding of tropical plants in land now arctic.

The prevalence of earthquakes the past few years is a warning of great changes to come. Changes for the coast-line of California have been prophesied by many who have made contact with the unseen. The destruction of New York city by earthquake has been foretold by Baha'u'llah and several other prophets. Washington and Montana in the west, New York and Massachusetts in the east, have all had hurricanes and earthquakes in the past five years. What year the earth changes foretold by prophets will take place is unknown. We are in the years when a 99, a 200, a 3,000, a 12,000, a 24,000, a 36,000, and a 72,000-year cycle overlap, but

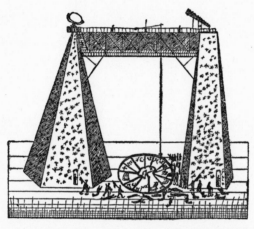

Observatory That Stood by the Great Pyramid of Osiris

a cycle of 33 years is such a small fraction of a cosmic day that it is impossible for us to tell at this time the exact year such changes may be expected. It requires a more profound knowledge of the mathematics of prophecy than is possessed by man in these early days of Kosmon. Before the next century has passed, however, science will open the rooms of the Great Pyramid, now unknown, and rediscover lost wisdom concerning cosmic cycles and their influence on human affairs.

The archives of the Essenes contain what purports to be a true account of the Great Pyramid and its builders. In this history we find the statement made that within the south (undiscovered) room of the Pyramid records are stored covering 3,000 years. Gathered from all inhabited sections of the earth, these records cover data pertaining to weather, wars, races, and other items used by the prophets in predicting the future.

This room is protected by unseen forces and will be guarded from discovery until world peace is established in 1948.

CHAPTER XV

SECRETS OF SYMBOLOGY AND ESOTERIC PSYCHOLOGY

SYMBOLOGY UNVEILED

The cross has, for many centuries, been recognized as a symbol distinctive of Christian peoples. As mankind progresses from birth to death, and as each new race appears, so also does the symbology of the race unfold. Physical, mental, and spiritual man is always denoted by a harmonious language, both spoken and written, and its accompanying symbology.

It is often remarked that anything can be proven by the Bible. Taken literally, much of the Bible is nonsense. Accepted for what it is, a compilation of inspired manuscripts dealing with the unfoldment of the human race, but written in the language of allegory, symbology, and astrology, it is a medium of spiritual and mental enlightenment.

Christianity is recognized, by those who have studied its source, as an outgrowth of the paganism of a past cycle. Christianity did not originate at the time the Nazarene lived, but came into being about three centuries later. Prior to that time, the cross had been used as a religious symbol, but carried a crucified lamb. Among the many symbols which the early Christians used to represent the main object of their faith, the lamb was the most predominant. At the beginning of the sixth century, the cross bears a lamb; later in the century, it is lying on the altar at the foot of the cross; still later, it appears with blood flowing from a wound in its side, as well as from its feet; and finally, by the end of the century, a lamb is painted in the center of the cross in the place where the body of Christ was later placed. On the celebrated cross of the Vatican, where this lamb appears are two portrayals of the Savior, one above, holding a book in the left hand and giving a benediction in the Latin manner with his right, the one below, holding a scroll in the right hand and a small cross in the left.

At the Sixth Ecumenical Council held at Constantinople in 680 A.D., it was ordained that in place of the lamb, the figure of a man should be portrayed on the cross. After this edict, the worship of a lamb on the cross was forbidden.

 As man progressed out of the dark ages, his worship changed from adoration of an animal to that of a man. During the past century the Unitarian faith, Christian Science, New Thought, Oxford Group (Buckmanites), and many others have been instruments to carry worship from a man born of woman to that of a god of spirit.

As we progress into the cycle of Kosmon, the Christian cross, as a religious symbol, will become obsolete, and the Kosmon cross of a new age will be adopted.

The Pope remarked when Hitler visited Mussolini not long ago, and the streets of Rome were decorated (or desecrated) with the cross of Hitler, that the swastika was not the cross of Christ. Hitler's cross is an atavistic cross of death, emblematical of the four dark forces. The one who knows the secrets of symbology can look at the insignia of a man or an order and know whether it be of light or dark, good or evil. A man reveals his mind by the symbols he adopts.

The Christian cross is a representation of the mankind of our Ghan race. Western peoples have used the cross for centuries, little realizing how significant it is of themselves and their mentalities. The cross symbolizes the three dimensional consciousness, and as mankind's mentality develops, so will his cross change from the unbalanced cross of the Christian to the balanced cross of Kosmon.

There are three phases to the mind of man: the subconscious, conscious, and super-conscious. The subconscious is the composite mind of all the cells of the body; the conscious is the mind of the self, I Am, or soul; the super-conscious is the mind of the spirit.

Into the consciousness of man two streams of impressions converge. From the subconscious come the demands of the physical man—his appetite, sex urge, physical desires of every sort and description, and a constant stream of impressions from his physical environment. The subconscious is the field of the physical. It is the mortal mind of the Christian Scientist, the animal mind.

Another stream of impressions flows in from the superconsciousness, which is the mind of the spirit. It is this phase of mind that we must thank for all original ideas, our faith, our intuition, our conscience, our religious ideals, our sense of right and wrong, for these are all impressions of a spiritual nature.

The subconscious functions over the solar-plexus and sympathetic nervous system, and centers in the back part of the brain. The conscious mind, or self-mind, operates over the cerebro-spinal nervous system and centers in the fore-brain. The super-conscious manifests through the pineal gland and top brain.

CHRISTIAN CROSS OF TODAY

```
                  THE
                 WITHIN
                   OR
                 UNSEEN
                  SUPER
                CONSCIOUS
  THE CONSCIOUS MIND.  IMPRESSIONS FLOWING INTO
  CONSCIOUSNESS ORIGINATE IN THE MORTAL MIND OF
  THE BODY OR ENTER OVER THE PHYSICAL SENSES FROM
  CORPOREAL ENVIRONMENT.
                  THE
                WITHOUT
                   OR
                  SEEN
                  SUB
                CONSCIOUS
                MORTAL MIND
                OF THE BODY
                 REALM OF
                 PHYSICAL
                APPETITES.
```

Each phase of consciousness has its own frequency and color. The subconscious is red, a low frequency. The conscious is yellow, an intermediate frequency. The superconscious is blue, a higher frequency.

186

When the cells of the body need nutriment a message travels over the sympathetic nervous system, at a low frequency, to the solar plexus where the impulse is converted into the intermediate frequency of consciousness. Only then does the individual become aware of hunger.

A mental impression of any kind outside the field of the physical body and its three dimensional environment is a message originating in the super, or spiritual, consciousness. When we have a new idea, have an impression that an action we are contemplating is wrong, or endeavor to recall a picture of some past event, each of these is a function of the super-conscious, and it manifests itself in the body as a nerve impulse of high frequency. When converted into the intermediate frequency of the conscious mind, we have an idea.

Thought is the weighing of a present problem on the scales of past experience. Consciousness is a medley of impressions from both the sub and super phases of mind.

Herein is the secret of mental telepathy or transference of thought from one person to another. You may have a thought that you wish to transmit to some loved one at a distance. If you are able to convert this thought into the higher frequency of the super-conscious, it is broadcast into the ether. This energy impinges on the superconscious, or spirit mind, of your friend. Only when he has reconverted the high frequency of the spirit, by means of his pineal gland, into the intermediate frequency of the conscious mind will he receive the message and be aware that you are *en rapport* or in tune with him.

Mental telepathy is a transference of mental pictures or visualizations, and not a transference of words. So if you would try a few experiments in thought transference, build a picture of the idea you wish to convey, and visualize your friend receiving this picture. You may be amazed at your success.

The conscious mind should be positive, the other two phases negative. The real self, the I AM, the Soul-Mind, should be the master. The Essene training develops this soul mastery whereby the initiate comes into full command of his body, his spirit and his environment.

The Master, Adept, Prophet, the true Essene, is a balanced man, a man who has attained the ability to command equally either the cells of his physical organism or the attributes of his spirit. He can direct his attention to any organ or part of his body and force it to do his will, or he can silence the appetites of his body and listen to the still small voice of the spirit. He can go into the "silence," to that kingdom of heaven to be found within. He is the super-man. If his attention is directed to a world without, he is master, for he has learned concentration of will and effort. If he directs his attention within, he is in command of his being and of every mental power. His is the four dimensional consciousness, the realization of the unseen world of spirit and the seen world of matter. His is the ability to contact the unseen infinite field of causation and the seen finite fields of effect. Past, present, future are within his ken. He has the ability to use the superior laws of spirit to overcome the inferior laws of matter.

The cross of Kosmon is the balanced cross of the balanced man, equal with respect to the powers of spirit, body, and intellect. The Master can stop the flow of

CROSS OF THE MASTER, PROPHET OR TRUE ESSENE.
The Cross of Tomorrow.

This man makes his own destiny and creates
his own environment.

```
                    ┌──────────────┐
                    │  SPIRITUAL   │
                    │      OR      │
                    │    SUPER-    │
                    │   CONSCIOUS  │
                    │     MIND     │
                    │              │
                    │     BLUE     │
          ┌─────────┤              ├─────────┐
          │                                   │
          │  SELF CONSCIOUSNESS, THE I AM OR SOUL MIND
          │  COGNIZES IMPRESSIONS OF THE SPIRIT EQUAL
          │  WITH THOSE OF THE BODY AND CORPOREAL WORLD.
          │                                   │
          │          GOLDEN YELLOW            │
          └─────────┤              ├─────────┘
                    │  CORPOREAL   │
                    │    MORTAL    │
                    │      OR      │
                    │     SUB-     │
                    │   CONSCIOUS  │
                    │     MIND     │
                    │              │
                    │     RED      │
                    └──────────────┘
```

This man has faith only in his Creator and
knows that he knows.

impressions coming into his mind from the physical
world without, and live in the spirit, or he can heed the
wise voice of his spiritual consciousness and concentrate
his powers on the world without.

189

CHAPTER XVI

THE MARK OF THE MASTER

Masons will note in the following symbolism a correspondence with their order.

The emblem of the Junior Warden is the plumb-line or perpendicular, while that of the Senior Warden is

Egyptian Masonry

the level or horizontal. The combination forms the perfect cross: the cross of the master. In Masonry it is symbolized by the square.

The swastika is made up of four squares placed in such a position that they denote the direction of travel from east to west. Wherever this cross is found it is evidence that the people who used it possessed the secrets of ancient Masonry and had wisdom schools similar to that of the Essenes. The swastika cross was known to all the Indian tribes. To them it was a symbol of the Creator, or Great Spirit, and of His works.

It has been found woven in silk and engraved on coins in China and Japan. It has been placed on coins, stoles and amulets in Mesopotamia. It has been hewn into stone in Egypt and Central America. The North American Indians wove it into their blankets and baskets, painted and carved it on wood. It is evidence that at one time every one of these people worshipped the Great Spirit or Architect of the Universe. It is a symbol of the I'hins, the mound-builders of North America.

The arms of the ancient swastika were always square with the world, pointed to the four light quarters of the universe, east, south, west, and north, and denoted a clockwise rotation as did the ancient astrological charts. In this position, the swastika

CROSS OF LIFE
Clockwise rotation
Square with the world

is a symbol of *light* and of travel from ignorance to wisdom. It denotes progression.

Hitler designed the flag of the Nazis, a flag with a background of red upon which is a white circle having in its center a black false swastika.

But note this carefully: he *reversed* the direction of rotation of the swastika and placed it pointing to the four dark corners of the universe, northeast, northwest, southeast, and southwest. In the ancient initiations, the four dark corners signified four evil forces. By changing the direction of rotation of the swastika from clockwise to counter-clockwise, he makes this ancient cross a symbol of travel from knowledge to ignorance, retrogression. This is evidenced in his exiling many of the best minds of Germany, and his destruction of the German universities that had so long enjoyed a reputation as the best.

CROSS OF DEATH
Counter-clockwise rotation
Cross bones—Poison

Placed in the position which the swastika occupies in the Nazi flag, the cross of the master is changed to the cross of death, the cross-bones, symbol of poison, darkness, evil, and destruction. It is then a *false*, not a true swastika.

Hitler is a psychic controlled by a god of force whose objective is chaos in the affairs of men. He is the destroyer. His work is the destruction of the competitive capitalistic system, international banking and national barriers, that they may be replaced by a system of co-operative effort. His rabid nationalism will destroy itself and will be replaced by a benign internationalism. By means of evil, he clears the way for good. His is a necessary work in the evolution of mankind.

Hitler is the wrecker; his the work of clearing the earth of old institutions so that new and better methods may replace them. He is the destroyer of international finance based upon banker-controlled gold; his the task of razing the Christian Church, whose birthplace is Rome. His part is that of instigating a world-wide anti-semitism that will purge the Jews of self and money

192

worship, and will separate the Jews from the Israelites, who worship the Creator only.*

Hitler occupies the place in this cycle of Kosmon that Pharaoh occupied three thousand years ago. As it took the oppression of the Egyptians to force the Israelites of old to leave a nation about to be destroyed, so has it taken the lashes of the Nazis to drive the Israelites from Germany. Their departure is, in itself, a prophecy of the destruction of the German Nation.

* Kindly note the difference between Jews and Israelites. The term "Jew" is commonly used in present day propaganda where Mammon, Babylon, or capitalism based upon the principle of usury is meant. The Jew is the antithesis of Israel. The Jew is an idol—a money-worshipper, while the Israelite is a monotheist and obeys the commandment, "Thou shalt have no other gods before me." The United States is the coming Israel. Our constitution forbids the power of the state to be used to support any religion. The Creator can manage His own creations without help from the state or church.

CHAPTER XVII

Interpretation of the Great Seal of the U. S. and Thirteen Cycles in American History

One of the most interesting things in the study of symbology is the constant adoption of symbols by people who do not in the least suspect what it is they are doing, and who have no idea of the meanings of the symbols which they adopt.

Prior to the year 1914, nations used some member of the animal kingdom as a symbol on their flags or national coat of arms, for example, an eagle, lion, bear or dragon. The unfoldment of the spirituality and intellect of mankind in these years of transition is evidenced by the change in their symbols.

Russia adopted the "Hammer and Sickle"—a symbol of labor in the Creator's vineyard. Germany adopted the reversed, or false swastika, an emblem of death or disintegration. The United States brought to light the reverse side of the Great Seal of the United States, and is now using both sides of the seal on dollar bills. The publication of this seal denotes a coming change in the religion, government, and economy of the nation. An interpretation of the symbolism of the Great Seal of the United States will reveal a prophecy of the future of our country.

The number four prominently appears in the history

of the United States. The Fourth of July is the date on which the order was given for the designing of this seal, and is also the date upon which the Declaration of Independence was signed. The number thirteen is an expansion of the number four, and appears throughout the history of our country. Thirteen is our national number.

There are thirteen bars in our flag and thirteen rods on our national mace. The inscription "Annuit Coeptis," meaning "He hath prospered our beginning," is made up of thirteen letters. The aura of light above the eagle's head contains thirteen stars arranged in a manner to form the interlocked triangles of the Star of David, or emblem of Israel. The eagle holds thirteen arrows in the right talon, and an olive branch of thirteen leaves in the left.

The Confederate flag contained thirteen stars, although there were never more than eleven states in the Confederacy. On the thirteenth day of the month, Fort Sumter was fired upon. Dewey took Manila on the thirteenth.

In the world war, the number thirteen appears again and again. Although Thomas Woodrow Wilson was the full name of the president who led us into war, he had shortened his name to thirteen letters, Woodrow Wilson. It took thirteen days for the thirteen vessels making up the first expedition to reach France. John J. Pershing, a general with thirteen letters in his name, commanded the U. S. forces in the first battle (Belleau Woods), occurring on June 13th.

The number thirteen made its appearance in our destiny before we were a nation, for thirteen generals of the Revolutionary War were Free Masons. Washington was Master of the Lodge.

The Declaration of Independence was drawn up largely by Masons and Masonic Lodges were the centers of activity preceding the War of Independence. The patriotic society, Cacus Pro Bono Publico, was made up of members of St. Andrews Lodge of Boston, and it was members of this society, disguised as Indians, who conducted the historic Boston Tea Party.

There is striking similarity between the symbols of Masonry and those appearing on the seal of the United States. Neither the name of Christ nor the term "Christian" are heard any place in the ritual of the Blue Lodge of Masonry, nor is any Christian symbol used in the original three degrees of Masonry. However, the terms "Architect of the Universe" and "God" are used many times, for no atheist can become a member of the Masonic Fraternity without perjuring himself.

The founders of our country were deeply religious men but were wise enough to forbid, in our Constitution, any state supported church. Possibly they foresaw the time when Christianity, in the endeavor to rule the world, would destroy itself to make way for a new universal religion based upon the worship of the Creator rather than worship of a savior.

The All Seeing Eye of the Creator is a Masonic symbol. This same symbol is prominent on the reverse side of the Great Seal, brought to light on the one dollar silver certificates first released to circulation December 18, 1935. Enclosed in a triangle, the emblem of office of God, who is chief executive officer governing our planet, this eye appears surrounded by an aura of light

196

above the pyramid. While it seems to be the cap stone of this pyramid, you will note that it is detached from the pyramid.

Many interpreters of the symbology of the U. S. seal have claimed that the All Seeing Eye is significant of Christ. Permit me to state unequivocally and posi-

The Seal of the United States

(REVERSE SIDE)

Annuit Coeptis,	Novus Ordo Seclorum,
"Prosper us in our undertaking."	"A New System of Ethics will arise."

tively that this is not correct. The All Seeing Eye is a symbol of the Creator and signifies his guardianship over this nation.

The eye looks down on a pyramid built of thirteen courses. On the bottom course is inscribed, MDCC-LXXVI, the date 1776. It is probable that the thirteen courses signify thirteen cycles in our national history of thirteen years each, a total of 169 years. A few of the events occurring during 169 years are listed. Only those occurrences are given which are outstanding in their effects on tomorrow.

The year 1945 marks the end of this series of thirteen cycles. With 1945 will come a great change in the government, economics, and religion of our nation. Then we shall see the fulfillment of the prophecy contained in the banner at the base of the pyramid, "Novus Ordo Seclorum," meaning the *NEW ORDER and GENERATIONS*.

The new order will not be a counterfeit New Deal, but will be God's Kingdom on earth brought into manifestation by the new generations of Kosmon. This prophecy is verified in the name of our continent, America. Prof. Miskovski of Oberlin College states that the word "America" seems to have been formed from the Gothic words "Amel Ric" meaning heavenly kingdom.

The archives of the Essenes contain a prophecy stating that Jehovah's kingdom, or the Kingdom of God on earth, will first be founded on this continent in the vicinity of Colorado. We can expect the first signs of its manifestation between 1945 and 1948.

SALIENT EVENTS IN AMERICAN HISTORY OCCURRING IN THIRTEEN CYCLES OF THIRTEEN YEARS EACH

1. 1776–1789. Thomas Payne's pamphlet "Common Sense."
   Declaration of Independence.
   National flag adopted 1777.
   U. S. independence recognized by France.
   First newspaper, the Philadelphia ADVERTISER, begins publication, 1784.
   Shay's rebellion of farmers against high taxes collected to redeem bonds sold to finance the war. Bondholders had received their money back in interest already paid.
   First presidential election and inauguration of Washington in 1789.

198

2. 1789–1802. Supreme Court founded.

Bank of the U. S. chartered by Congress in 1791.

Washington's farewell address in 1796, in which he emphatically warned the country against foreign entanglements.

3. 1802–1815. Louisiana Purchase in 1803.

War with Great Britain in 1812.

4. 1815–1828. Congress charters second Bank of the U. S.

1819 first steamship crosses the Atlantic.

Declaration of the Monroe Doctrine in 1822.

1828 first protective tariff passed.

5. 1828–1841. Second Bank of the U. S. passes out of existence, 1832.

First railroad started operation.

Money panic of 1837 due to issuance of notes by wildcat banks.

Telegraph patented in 1840.

Sub-Treasury bill passed making the Federal government the depository of its own funds.

6. 1841–1854. Joseph Smith, founder of Mormon Church, murdered at Carthage, Ill. June 27, 1844.

Brigham Young leads migration to Utah in 1847.

Gold discovered in California in 1848.

Commodore Perry opens Japan to commerce.

Birth of the Kosmon Era in 1848.

7. 1854–1867. First oil well drilled in Pennsylvania in 1859.

Civil War 1861–65.   Chattel slavery abolished.

Bill enacted in 1862 authorizing issuance of paper money (greenbacks) in place of interest bearing bonds.

Atlantic cable completed.

8. 1867–1880. Big business born during this cycle.

Atlantic and Pacific coasts joined by rail, 1869.

Telephone patented in 1876.

Electric light invented in 1879.

9. 1880–1893. Founding of American Red Cross, 1881.

Sherman Antitrust law passed in 1890.

Standard Oil trust ordered dissolved in 1892.

Industrial unrest, strikes, and military action against labor prevalent during this cycle.

10. 1893–1906. Panic of 1893 brought on more labor troubles.
Coxey's army marches on Washington, 1894.

J. P. Morgan strengthens his hold on the government of the U. S. with a loan of $62,000,000 at 4%.

Election of William McKinley was a victory for Wall Street, and initiated an era of imperialism and industrial control of the U. S.

Edison invented motion picture camera in 1897.

U. S. declares war on Spain, 1898.

Gold standard established in 1900.

Wright brothers invent airplane in 1903.

11. 1906–1919. War of Armageddon started in Europe in 1914 with a thirty-three year cycle of disaster.

San Francisco fire and earthquake, 1906.

Money panic of 1907.

Titanic sinks in 1912 with a loss of over 1,000 lives.

Infamous Federal Reserve Act passed in 1913, giving privately owned banks license to issue money.

Ludlow massacre of miners by troops in Colorado, 1914.

Influenza epidemic of 1918 killed hundreds of thousands.

Armistice, Nov. 11, 1918.

First flight across the Atlantic in 1919.

12. 1919–1932. The twelfth thirteen year cycle brings the harvest from evil seed sown by the rule of bankers and big business. Organized crime copied the methods of bankers and corporations and gave us an epidemic of gangsters.

1924 reveals the Doheny-Fall oil scandal.

Superintendent of Anti-Saloon league convicted of forgery. Attorney General Harry L. Daugherty is requested to resign. Governor McCray of Indiana convicted of mail fraud. Thomas W. Miller, former Alien Property Custodian, convicted of conspiracy to defraud the government.

Herbert Hoover elected president in 1928.

Panic of 1929. Wave of wage cuts started by steel trust.

Franklin D. Roosevelt elected president.

13. 1932–1945. Closing of the banks and birth of the New (?) Deal.

Dictatorial powers voted Roosevelt in 1933 to cope with banking and financial crisis. Ownership of gold money outlawed.

Investigation of J. P. Morgan & Co. by Senate committee, but nothing comes of it.

U. S. Senate Committee investigates the munition and armament industry, 1934. Another dud.

1936 to 1940 sees march of Fascism-Nazism in Europe and second session of War of Armageddon. Roosevelt and Hull following in footsteps of Wilson and Lansing on the path to war.

Election of American Dictator in 1940. Second Civil War of 1944. Release from bondage to the bankers.

CHAPTER XVIII

Comparison of Communism and Fascism

The terms "communism," "Fascism" and "Nazism" have been used a countless number of times in newspapers, periodicals, and on the radio during the last decade. It is astonishing how few people have ever taken the time or trouble to consider the real meanings of the terms and to clarify their understanding of the ambitions of each pertaining to government and economy.

The average newspaper reader has the idea that communism and Nazi-Fascism are synonymous terms representing similar ideologies, when in fact they are terms representing cultures as opposite as black and white. Writers in our capitalistic magazines have made little, if any, effort to clarify the subject, and seem more desirous of misleading the public than informing them of the truth.

The ideal of the communist is a *classless society* wherein there will no longer exist an excessively rich few at the top, nor poverty stricken millions at the bottom, but a new class will be formed, including all the world's peoples living in an economy of abundance wherein there shall be plenty for all. The capitalist and industrialist have always fought and will continue to fight this ideal, for only by an economy based upon scarcity and high prices can he maintain his excessive riches and power.

As Hitler is the supreme Nazi-Fascist, we will look to him for enlightenment on the ambitions and ideals of his party. It will consist of an elite ruling class with Hitler the supreme pontiff. Hitler voiced his ideal government in a statement to Hermann Rauschnigg, a translation of which follows:

There will be a ruling caste tempered by battle, and assembled from various elements. This group will be the hierarchy of the party. There will be an intermediate class of the anonymous, the serving collective, the eternally disfranchised, no matter whether they formerly belonged to the bourgeoisie, the big land-owning class, the workers, or the craftsman. Beneath them there will be another class of the alien subject races. We will call them the slave class.

The reader will note that the ambitions and objectives of the Nazi-Fascists are the antithesis of those of the communists. To aid the reader in comprehending the similarities and antagonisms between the two ideologies, they have been compared in their functions in the columns that follow:

COMPARISON OF COMMUNISM AND FASCISM-NAZISM

Communism

Fascism-Nazism

RULED BY DICTATORSHIP of the Proletariat. Parliamentary form of government abolished, and industrial form of government set up. Government operated through "soviets" or *councils*. President and Secretary of the party are servants of the people who rule from the bottom up through the soviets.

RULED BY DICTATOR, financed by the bankers and large industrialists (the HAVES). Used as a counter-offensive against Communism by the Owner-Rulers.

203

A CORPORATE STATE in the form of a cooperative commonwealth in which each citizen owns his share of all the collective wealth: lands, mines, factories, railroads, etc. Each worker is entitled to an equal share in profits which are distributed as collective benefits—unlimited educational advantages, health care, rest homes, recreational centers, provisions for sickness and disability, etc.

FARMS, FACTORIES, MINES, TOOLS OF PRODUCTION AND ALL REAL WEALTH are owned cooperatively by all the people and operated for the use and benefit of all. No exploitation of labor.

UNION membership is almost obligatory. The union is held in highest esteem in the U. S. S. R. Through their unions the industrial form of government is attained and the worker takes an active part in all government. All members of the Communist Party MUST belong to a labor union. The "soviets" are created through a union. The supreme soviet is made up of members selected by the soviets. The worker thus has a close, personal contact with the Supreme Council through his local soviet whose position in this council depends solely on the vote of the workers

A CORPORATE STATE that has taken control of income from capital. By a system of taxation and levies against capital, the state tends to level off great wealth. It has an equalizing effect; the wealthy cease to be so rich, and the condition of the poorer classes is materially benefited. The U. S. A., with its income and inheritance taxes, and relief projects, is approaching this state.

LAND, FACTORIES, AND TOOLS OF PRODUCTION owned by capitalistic class but the state takes the profit. Production for war takes precedence over production for peace or the needs of the people.

UNIONS are destroyed that the individual may have no means for collective protest or action other than that dictated. Every vestige of democracy vanishes with destruction of the labor unions.

in their districts or union. All representatives draw salaries equal to the wages of the skilled laborer. There are no lobbies and no padded expense accounts.

YOUTH. Full educational advantages open to all. Drilled from infancy in Marx's economic theories that they may bring into manifestation a classless society with equal opportunities for all. The horrors and inequalities of capitalism explained and possibly exaggerated.

STANDARD OF LIVING in terms of bathtubs, not as good as America's middle class or skilled worker, but neither did America have plumbing when it was less than twenty-five years old. Starting from huts and slums less than twenty-five years ago, the standard of living is being raised year by year. The great need for industrial development held their housing projects back, so Russians are greatly over-crowded in cities and towns.

WAR has not been an objective of the U. S. S. R. Several times they have tried to come to an agreement with other countries for general disarmament, but were blocked by England. They have foreseen the time when the Capitalist nations would gang up to destroy the new government and economy, and have been

YOUTH is given training only in those things which add to the nation's war power. Taught more lies than truth. Permitted to think only as dictator wishes.

STANDARD OF LIVING was slowly being improved until outbreak of war in Sept. 1939. Thereafter living conditions rapidly became worse. Real wages decreased. Motto now: "Bullets before butter," "Battleships before bread."

WAR is objective of have-not nations to get needed land for colonies and raw materials to keep factories in operation. Imperialism and aggression are major characteristics of all capitalistic and Fascist nations. Have nations, like Have people, resent ambition in Have-Nots.

205

forced, in self-defense, to arm. Their conquest of Finland was to prevent this country being used as a base of attack by other countries. The section of Finland seceded to the U. S. S. R. was needed by her as time will prove.

PLANNED ECONOMY. No country in the world had a planned economy until the U. S. S. R. inaugurated it. The Planning Board is selected by the Supreme Soviet, and is composed of scientific research workers, architects, engineers, statisticians, economists, agricultural experts. Each works in his own field to perfect plans that will give each citizen a more abundant life, greater opportunities, better health, more cultural advantages. Production is planned that greatest good and wisest use may be had from land and tools. Work for everyone.

PLANNED ECONOMY is concentrated for war purposes rather than abundance for everyone. Both Mussolini and Hitler have made honest efforts to provide work and raise the living standards of the common people. Like all capitalist countries, especially England and the U. S. A., the little economic planning that is done is for war. Any war that is engaged in will be either to protect the interests of the owner-rulers or to destroy the new cooperative economy. Everyone employed, largest percent in activities related to war.

EDUCATION controlled by the state. Literacy raised 85%. Books and publications widely distributed. Special attention given to music, the arts, and literature. Educational advantages limited only by the individual's ability to progress. All fields open. Youth is trained from earliest childhood to think in terms of social welfare rather than individual benefit.

EDUCATION is state controlled. Books are burned, publications suppressed that only teaching endorsed by the dictator may reach the eyes and ears of the people. Illiteracy increased. Education for war primarily. Youth educated to think in terms of rabid nationalism.

Communism	Fascism-Nazism

SCIENCE. Research unhampered and encouraged. Medicine, agriculture, aviation, and exploring greatly benefited. Costs for this are reckoned for in the planned economy, and come under the head of benefits for all.

SCIENTIFIC RESEARCH is restricted to that which will increase war power of the nation.

RELIGION similar to the U. S. A. in that there is no church recognized by the state. In Moscow there are Christian, Jewish, and Mohammedan Churches. No state aid is given to them. If members want them they must support them. Adults free to worship as they please, but in schools children are given anti-Christian teaching. Children receive strict teaching as to morals and behavior. Because the Communist Party broke the strangle-hold of the Greek Catholic Church which had fought it and betrayed the people again and again, because the Church fell to pieces when its organized racket was broken up, the U. S. S. R. has been maligned about its attitude toward religion.

RELIGION that of ROME. Both Mussolini and Hitler are Roman Catholics and affiliated with the Vatican.

Communism represents the positive progressive pole, Fascism * the negative reactionary pole, democracy (so called) the neutral. The U. S. A., England, France, and the Scandinavian countries claim to be democracies,

* Nazism is an outgrowth of Fascism. Nazism is the German brand, Fascism the Italian brand of the same thing. Today, in the United States, it is frequently termed "Christian Americanism," or some similar term acceptable to the unthinking.

but partake of the characteristics of both cooperative communism and competitive Fascism.

As negative flows to positive, so does the force of circumstances change Fascism into communism. This is illustrated in Germany. Hitler damned communism for years. Fritz Thyssen, the richest industrialist of Germany, financed Hitler and his party in the early days, expecting to pull the strings to actively guide Hitler, and insure his own position as owner and real ruler. But Thyssen found that Hitler could not be controlled, but on the contrary confiscated all of the Thyssen wealth. Herein is a lesson for our sixty families, a lesson which they should, but will not, heed.

Hitler preached the conquest and destruction of the U. S. S. R. It is one objective he will never attain. The communist state does the job of re-distributing the land and wealth directly; the Fascist state accomplishes the same result by a slower and more indirect method.

The men of the House of Have are but kidding themselves when they think that they can destroy communism by financing Fascist dictators in their wars. They but speed the change and destroy themselves. The conflict between the Communist and Fascist schools of thought is the War of Armageddon and will be the means by which the millennium, a thousand years of peace on earth, good will to men, will be ushered in. Then, indeed, will Christian prayers be answered and a kingdom come on earth as it is in heaven.

The Creator's Clock is striking twelve to mark a thousand year recess for the workers of the world. Not much longer can the owner-rulers withhold plenty—in a land of plenty—from the people who produce that plenty. Selfishness, like every other evil or negative condition, is self-destroying.

In the destruction of self, as embodied in the governments of today, we will witness the death of three blood brothers: finance, church, and state. These three are symbolized in Masonic ritual as the three ruffians; Jubala, Jubalo, and Jubalum, the last letters of each name making AOM, the negative principle of the Creator. As these three ruffians killed and buried the Master Mason of long ago, so will the trinity—finance, church, and capitalist state—kill the embryonic democracies of the world.

But as Hiram was resurrected by the grip of the Lion's Paw, so will the nations recover a new life through the discovery of the TRUE lost word, JEHOVAH, the I AM, Architect of the Universe. With unity of religion will come unity of government, unity of exchange, and unity of freedom.

Babylon, a term used in the Bible to denote chaos; finance, with its gold and silver standards; religion with its Christian, Mohammedan, Brahman, and Buddhist churches; the state with its monarchies, democracies, and dictatorships—all these will go down, to be replaced by God's kingdom on earth, a cooperative mutualism where each shall live in peace and plenty and no longer go out to produce for another while his children starve.

CHAPTER XIX

Fascism in California

A history of the labor movement and the age-old struggle between the dispossessed worker and the owner-ruler class was written half a century ago by G. Osborne Ward, then librarian of the U. S. Department of Labor. In this book, "The Ancient Lowly, a History of the Ancient Working People," Ward proves by innumerable translations of inscriptions, records, and archeological discoveries of the nineteenth century that the world-wide wars of today are based upon the same causes as the smaller wars of yesterday, that they are, in a word, *economic!*

The wars in Europe and Asia are part of the same struggle along national lines as that which has occurred and is still going on from an economic standpoint in our own California. Here in the short history of a state we see a recapitulation of the history of capital and labor, the rich versus the poor, which was going on even in Jesus' time.

John Steinbeck in "Of Mice and Men" and his "Grapes of Wrath" portrayed the grim story in fiction, while Carey McWilliams, Commissioner of Immigration and Housing in California, tells the story of California's workers and poor in a non-fiction book, "Factories in the Field," based on investigations of his commission. The story of the suffering of the poor, of course, is not a new story. Charles Dickens gave it to us in "Oliver Twist," Victor Hugo in "Les Miserables," Paul de Kruif in "Why Keep Them Alive," Helen Hunt Jackson in "Ramona," and Harriet Beecher Stowe in "Uncle Tom's Cabin." Yet such a story has always stirred the heart of humanity, and from time to time something is done to mitigate the tragedy and suffering, for the world grows a little better, a degree kinder.

"Factories in the Field" is a brilliant example of history as it should be written. Too many times history is but a recital of war aims and accomplishments of the ruling class, thickly padded with propaganda to "sell" this dominant class to posterity. In other words, most history is the written accomplishment of press agents working in the interests of the "robber barons."

McWilliams makes a radical departure, and instead of painting a Pollyanna picture of wars, battles, generals, a story of conquests and glory of "bandits" working within the law, he draws a picture of the systematic looting of the state, its lands, treasures, and workers, by the ruling class. The evidence is there—although he doesn't point it out—that "democracy" as the world knows it today is but the legislative arm of the owning or capitalistic class. Karl Marx, in 1848, said, "The capitalistic state is the defender, by force of arms, of the power and wealth of the ruling class." No greater proof of this statement could be asked than is presented in the history of California—"Factories in the Field."

No other state in the Union possessed from the beginning all of the factors which so ably contributed to the building of Fascism as California. Where the Anglo-Saxons in the eastern part of the United States killed, dispossessed and drove back the Indian, the Spaniards fought, crushed and dispossessed the native Indian, and then converted him into a sort of slave, a peon. Then came the discovery of gold in '48–49, and with it came those who found California a going feudal state with the vast estates of Spanish grandees set amidst a virgin wilderness. Great and sudden wealth, together with the lawlessness attendant in a gold rush, enabled the few at the top not only to seize rich gold holdings of smaller men but to buy outright, almost intact, the huge land estates of the Spanish grandees.

The coming of the railroads enabled this same clique to make large land grabs, to loot public land grants, and from 1850 to dominate the state. Governors, senates, legislatures, courts, schools, and colleges all came under their rule. They went further, for they owned the press of the state, dominated public opinion, suppressed any damaging truth, and always played up their own side of every controversy. Fascism, as early as 1850, took the place of Spanish feudalism.

Public opinion is very apt to be a canned article—made and processed by the press. During the very years when Czarist Russia was held up to Americans as the country where farm workers were forced to live in the most degrading, horrible poverty, when the well-known tyranny of the old Czars made Americans feel that America was a glorious, free, rich country, and that Russia was a most cruel and backward country, right then, worse conditions of poverty, looting, and degradation were in full bloom here in our own United States, and of all places, California!

But because these looters owned the press, legislature,

the courts, *none* of these dark facts—not a whisper of this black history—leaked out, and people thought of the state as the Chamber of Commerce and the Southern Pacific wanted them to think of it.

It was natural, therefore, that California should attract some of the most Utopian-minded people that have ever lived in America. Among these were the founders of the old Kaweah Co-operative Colony who took up government land, all properly filed on, and established a prosperous colony which became known throughout the United States and much of Europe. McWilliams tells this story in detail, supporting his charges by the records.

The two founders, Burnette G. Haskell, a young lawyer from San Francisco, and J. J. Martin, active in the labor movement, became convinced after reading a book, "The Co-operative Commonwealth," by Laurence Gronlund, that more could be accomplished by withdrawing from society and founding a co-operative colony, than could be accomplished by working in and through labor unions. They interested a group of high-minded people and together they took up about 600 acres of wooded land which at the time was thirty miles from the nearest town. They carefully figured out a road, through mountains, valleys, and canyons, which if built would shorten the distance to eighteen miles. They pitched a tent city and commenced the work of constructing the road. An average of twenty men worked continually for four years building this road, which wound through canyons and crossed mountains at elevations of 8,000 feet. They raised $50,000 by subscription to put into this project, and issued work checks for $150,000.

So well did they construct this road that it is in use today.

During these four years, the colonists endured great hardships and privations to which they submitted cheerfully, feeling that they were building a new and better society, a co-operative commonwealth in which poverty would be abolished.

When the road was completed, they laid out the town of Kaweah, allotting plots of 55 square yards for each homesite.

In 1892, William Carey Jones of the University of California, visited the place and reported very favorably, saying that he found the people fine, intelligent, cultured, charming, and many of them very brilliant. The colonists loved music and art, gave many concerts, and during the four years of the colony's existence there was no crime, lawlessness, or misdemeanors of any sort.

At the end of four years this colony, which varied in population from fifty to three hundred people, was free of debt, owned property worth $600,000 net, owned and operated a saw-mill worth $10,000, a tractor and turbine, and equipment to construct a planing mill, a shingle mill, and a woolen mill. It possessed the best printing press in California and printed its own weekly magazine, which circulated throughout the United States and in Europe. They constructed a ferry, and owned, besides these things, homes, furnishings, live-stock, wagons, and other farm implements.

The colonists prospered. They were growing. They were happy. More, they were proving to the whole world that a co-operative colony can be a success. It was all something to make the ruling class very unhappy.

They decided to build a railroad eighteen miles long

to the nearest town. It was as though the gardener had decided to wear the king's crown, for railroads in the United States are quite the most peculiar form of private property that we have. A good orthodox, capitalistic railroad is built first by huge land grants given to the company by the government of all the people, and this is added to by land obtained through various shady transactions. Next, millions of dollars of watered stock is sold to the public; and last and most important, the government itself pours in millions of dollars to keep the railroads going.

The innocent might think that because the people's money (for what else is government money?) built and maintains these roads that the people would own them—but no! The people's money built them, but a small capitalist class owns them.

This economic juggling of the capitalist reveals just why, when these colonists planned to build a road themselves, using their own money and labor, and owning it co-operatively, they were setting a dangerous precedent. They were about to let the cat out of the bag about railroads.

Sheer heresy could not be allowed, and it was not. Rushing to Washington as a hungry child runs to its wet-nurse, the capitalists of California introduced a bill in Congress and railroaded it through the Senate, making the colonists' land into a NATIONAL PARK—none other than SEQUOIA NATIONAL PARK.

The capitalist class has long pointed the finger of scorn, contempt, and hatred at Karl Marx, but they would have done better for themselves had they read his writings, and saved themselves the embarrassment of

215

following the exact lines of the pattern which he said was theirs. The rest of this story proves Marx's contention that the government is the legislative arm of the ruling class, and that the courts and army are maintained to enforce the property rights, wealth, and power of this group. This leads to the conclusion that the citizen can have no legal or constitutional rights which conflict with the interests of the ruling class. The rest of the story of the colony would seem to bear this out.

The "robber barons," who put the U. S. Government itself to work to confiscate the private property of its own people, trumped up as excuses the charges that the land had not been filed on properly, that the colonists had damaged the land and were destroying the trees.

The colonists protested against these charges, and a government official, U. S. Commissioner L. A. Groff, was sent to investigate. He found and reported that the filings were correct and in perfect order; that they had careful plans under way for conservation and reforestation; that they had been of great service to the timber, caring for it and protecting it from fire and damage over a period of five years.

By the testimony of the government's own agent, all the charges against these people were found to be fraudulent; and yet, despite this proof, the Act of Congress for evicting these people stood. They were promptly kicked out, and their property and their total investment representing five years of hard work was confiscated.

This should have been enough, but the ruling class, when the theories of its ownership are challenged, becomes bestial in its cruelty and lust for revenge.

One of their saw-mills was located on private property, and when the colonists refused to leave, they were rounded up like criminals and driven away by the United States cavalry. Next they were dragged into court and convicted of cutting timber on government property! Then they were brought into court to answer to the charge of using the mails to defraud. U. S. District Judge Ross, however, ordered their acquittal, and made a very nice speech in their behalf.

It is a fact that they proved their innocence on all the charges trumped up against them, but it did them very little good. Their old friend, William Carey Jones of the University of California, also defended them, saying that a great injustice had been done to a most worthy group of people, and he cited the fact that large tracts of land, both valuable timber and good agricultural tracts, had been taken up by the railroads and large corporations not only illegally, but with the actual connivance of the government.

And now, having crushed, dispossessed, and persecuted these people to the full extent of the law, these same rulers turned their press loose upon them. These misguided people had proved beyond all doubt that cooperatives must fail, that "socialism" could not succeed! Even as late as 1928, thirty-six years later, a paper of the California press ran a series of articles about this venture to prove how doomed to failure were cooperative or socialistic ventures. The record seems to prove that this is true, *not* for the reasons given, but for the same reasons that Jews do not thrive in Germany!

This brings up the thought: granted that Hitler is an inhuman brute, that he has confiscated the property of Jews, run them out of their homes, and indulged in

217

many cruelties, but was he the first to commit crimes against the weak?

McWilliams tells of the various methods pursued by the rulers of California in acquiring their vast land holdings—a blood curdling story of crime, looting, graft—another chapter in America's story of the "robber barons."

The cultivation of these vast estates, running as they did from 10,000 to nearly 50,000 acres, brought a new development to American capitalism, what McWilliams calls "factories in the field." American agriculture, for the first time, was put on the basis of big business. Even the casual stranger is surprised, when he comes to California, to see vast farms stretching as far as the eye can reach, but no "farmhouse"! There is no comfortable home, surrounded by cow barns and out-buildings, chickens, dogs, and children, giving evidence of the usual American farmer's genial way of living. None of these things. Just acres upon acres of garden truck, berries, or wheat—a few human scarecrows bending low over the ground—but farmer homes there are none!

It is small wonder that California went into hostile action over John Steinbeck's book, "Grapes of Wrath," for the story of labor on the big farms in California is quite the most brutal, cruel story that has ever been lived out by the worker in all of labor's long, heartrending struggle.

The labor class, back in the early '50's, was composed of two totally different peoples: the Chinese coolie and the American drifter, or, often, hobo. The Chinese had been brought in and used to help construct the railroads, and after the railroads were completed, they were shifted to the mines. They were later run out of the mines, and then became a persecuted racial minority. The poor whites hated the Chinaman because he was an economic threat. They needed desperately the jobs he held. The ruling class played up this race hatred in their press because it made the Chinese more tractable. The Chinese had no legal rights, and could even be murdered with impunity. Eventually, they were driven from the farms into the city.

The American "drifter" for the most part, belonged to the "49'ers." He had become reduced to pauperism either because he had failed to discover any gold, or else had been swindled out of his mining claim. Some had come out as farmers, but had been swindled out of their land.

After the banishment of the Chinese, all sorts of cheap foreign labor was imported: Greek, Hindu, Jap, Filipino, Mexican. The Japanese outnumbered the others, and, excepting the Americans, caused the most trouble. A stranger coming into the state is amazed at the suspicion and the bitterness manifested toward a race of people who seem to him very polite, friendly, and kindly. If this stranger happens to be a cosmopolitan sort of person, or if he happens to believe in the brotherhood of man, he is likely to feel that in this mass display of race hatred there is a "nigger in the woodpile." There is, and a very big one, a stinking one, and for the first time in California's history, this "nigger" is revealed by McWilliams in his story of the State's labor, "Factories in the Field."

The story is too good to be told briefly and secondhand. The reader should read McWilliams' own account, but in brief, the story is this. The Japs were the only people ever to come to California who were clever enough to outsmart California's land barons. One of the great tragedies of California farm workers is the seasonal nature of crops. Two, three months, and the crop is over, the work gone. Another crop is hundreds of miles distant. The Japs were the first to meet this difficulty scientifically. They organized (crime of crimes to the rulers, always), and by the aid of a central bureau were able to find work and be transported to the next crop. Thus by working throughout the entire year, they were enabled to stretch out the miserable wage for which all farm labor is forced to work in California. Traveling about as they did, they were also able to locate tracts of land which they might buy or lease. It is true that often they got only the most undesirable land, sometimes land deemed entirely worthless, but the Japanese possessed an agricultural skill and knowledge that enabled them to take worthless land and grow luxuriant crops on it.

All of these things infuriated the land barons who, until that time, had had everything their own way, and were, in fact, the undisputed "lords of creation." To top all of this, the organized Japs would strike just when a perishable crop was ready to be harvested and there was no time to import strike-breakers. If this seems contemptible, we must remember that when the Japanese were "invited" to enter California they worked for as little as thirty-five to forty cents per day, and less, out of which they had to board themselves and pay their own transportation, while the owners were making $2,000,-000 on one or two crops.

The rapidity with which the Japanese were able to enlarge their tracts of land into profitable large holdings, their absorption of Japanese labor, the rise to wealth of these foreign land-owners who undersold the American corporation farmers—all these things contributed to the hatred of the white owning class for the Japanese. Infuriated, they turned their press and the mechanism of their government loose to arouse race hatred against these foreigners.

But let us see what kind of people these were who were stirring up so much race hatred against the Japanese.

McWilliams points to records which show that such organizations as the Salvation Army, Boy and Girl Scouts, a Presbyterian Church, state agencies, relief rolls, detention schools, and even public schools aided the land owners to exploit the weak, the destitute, the helpless.

Perhaps even worse than the brutal persecution of racial minorities, was the heartless exploitation of white Americans.

Detention schools kept two-fifths of each boy's earnings, the boys themselves keeping three-fifths. For a season's work, such boys earned for themselves from $20.00 to $50.00. By such methods, the owners boasted that they had produced a $2,000,000 grape and prune crop at a labor cost of $20,000. Deaf mutes were taken out of their schools and sent to work in the fields when the fruit crop alone was worth $235,000,000. All this wealth for a few owners, while workers were making only $2 and $3 per week and trying to support families on such a wage. It is no wonder that reports revealed that children, white children, American children, as young as five years old, were found working in cotton fields.

It has long been the boast of American capital that the American standard of living for the worker is the highest in the world. Roosevelt refers blandly to "the American way of living." This remark almost proves that he has never read "Grapes of Wrath" nor "Factories in the Field." Let us see how high this so-called high standard of living is for the American farm workers in California.

McWilliams says that in 1938–39 investigation showed that forty-one people were living in a two-room shack. Workers with no shelter were forced in cold weather to sleep on manure piles to keep warm. Workers were found to be living in shacks built of linoleum and cardboard, of tin and ragged pieces of carpet. Thousands of them in some of these camps had no drinking water except that found in stagnant pools. Some of the "houses" were nothing but gunny sacks stretched from trees to poles.

Through page after page McWilliams reveals the sickening horrors of the poverty forced upon workers—American workers—by the owners of these vast agricultural areas from which these owners reap millions of dollars a year. At their worst, neither the old Czar of Russia nor Hitler could have forced more horrible conditions upon the unfortunates of their lands than is endured by the American migrant farm worker in California.

Who and what are these people who are called "the migrant workers"? For the most part, they are the refugees of the "dust bowl." Of American stock, they

222

come from Kansas, Texas, Oklahoma. They have bat-
tled long years with drought, depression, despair, and
then finally the dust. Today they are broken Americans: Americans crushed by poverty, housed in filth
and vermin, and filled with despair. These are the people who, because of these things, are sneeringly referred
to as "migrant labor." Hoover, who has so much to say
of his great sympathy for the Finns, keeps silent before
the sorrows and wrongs of these fellow-countrymen,
these Americans, these workers within his own state!

Yet all men are not like Hoover. Long ago, an artist
looked upon a French peasant and made himself immortal by giving the world a picture of this broken,
worn peasant as he saw him. Later a poet, Edwin Mark-
ham, gazing on Millet's "Man With the Hoe" wrote
what today can be so well said of the California peasant:

> Bowed by the weight of centuries he leans
> Upon his hoe and gazes on the ground,
> The emptiness of ages on his face,
> And on his back the burden of the world.
> Who made him dead to rapture and despair,
> A thing that grieves not and never hopes,
> Stolid and stunned, a brother to the ox?
> Who loosened and let down this brutal jaw?
> Whose was the hand that slanted back this brow?
> Whose breath blew out the light within this brain?
>
>   *   *   *
>
> Is this the Thing the Lord God made and gave
> To have dominion over land and sea?
>
>   *   *   *
>
> O, Masters, lords and rulers in all lands,
> Is this the handiwork you give to God,
> This monstrous thing distorted and soul-quenched?
> How will you ever straighten up this shape;
> Touch it again with immortality,

Give back the upward looking and the light;
Rebuild in it the music and the dream;
Make right the immemorial infamies,
Perfidious wrongs, immediate woes?

O, Masters, lords and rulers in all lands
How will the Future reckon with this Man?
How answer his brute question in that hour
When whirlwinds of rebellion shake the world?
How will it be with kingdoms and with kings—
With those who shaped him to the thing he is—
When this dumb Terror shall reply to God
After the silence of the centuries?
       (Edwin Markham's "Man With The Hoe.")

Today the immense farms of California are owned by corporations which operate with the sole objective of extracting the greatest revenue from the land, and the most work for the least wages from the men who labor on the land. No matter what the fruit of the land may be, its greatest harvest today is private profit.

Within the next seven years the Associated Farms will be the Co-operative Farms, all owned by one mammoth corporation—the Corporation of the United States of America. Then the fruit of the land will feed a happy, contented, prosperous nation. California's greatest harvest will be happy, well-fed children. However, a dark night of strife, revolution and chaos lies between today and tomorrow.

CHAPTER XX

AMERICA: YESTERDAY, TODAY AND TOMORROW

At least three farsighted presidents of the United States foresaw the present condition of society.

Thomas Jefferson, author of the Declaration of Independence, said:

> If the American people ever allow private banks to control the issue of currency, first by inflation, and then by deflation, the banks and corporations that will grow up around them will deprive the people of all their property until their children will wake up homeless on the continent their fathers conquered.

James Madison, fourth president, said:

> We are free today, substantially, but the day will come when our republic will come to impossibility because its wealth will be concentrated in the hands of a few. When that day comes, then we must rely upon the wisdom of the best elements in the country to readjust the laws of the nation to the changed conditions.

Abraham Lincoln, sixteenth president, at the conclusion of the Civil War, said:

> I see in the future a crisis approaching that unnerves me and causes me to tremble for the safety of my country. As a result of war, corporations have been enthroned and an era of corruption in high places will follow. The *money power* will endeavor to prolong its reign by working on the prejudices of the people until all the wealth is aggregated into a few hands and the republic is destroyed.

The astonishing foresight of early presidents was recognized by Woodrow Wilson when he was in office, for he said:

The masters of the government of the United States are the combined capitalists and manufacturers of the United States.

The government of the United States at present is a foster child of the special interests. It is not allowed to have a will of its own.

The government, which was designed for the people, has gotten into the hands of bosses and their employers, the special interests. An invisible empire has been set up above the forms of democracy.

America is not a place of which it can be said, as it used to be, that a man may choose his own calling and pursue it as far as his abilities enable him to pursue it.

American industry is not free as once it was free; American enterprise is not free.

We have restricted credit, we have restricted opportunity, we have controlled development, and we have come to be one of the worst ruled, one of the most completely controlled and dominated governments in the civilized world—no longer a government by free opinion, no longer a government by conviction and the vote of the majority, but a government by the opinion and duress of small groups of dominant men.

The condition described by Wilson during his time became much worse in the years following the first World War. Today we find the wealth of the nation concentrated into the hands of some sixty families who represent the system of entrenched privilege and political reaction that is aggressively attacking the democratic rights of the American people. The needs of the people demand a fundamental revision of the economic, social, and legal structure, but a coalition of the most reactionary forces will resist any constructive change until they precipitate a second civil war.

The struggle of the people against these sixty families was clarified in a broadcast entitled: "It Is Happening Here," by Secretary of the Interior Ickes. He said:

Here in America it is the old struggle between the power of money and the power of the democratic instinct. In the last few months this irreconcilable conflict, long growing in our history, has come into the open as never before, has taken on a form and an intensity which makes it clear that it must be fought through to a finish . . . until plutocracy or democracy—until America's sixty families, or until America's 130,000,000 people win.

Economic power in this country does not rest in the mass of the people as it must if a democracy is to endure. Wealth is not equitably distributed nor do its owners in the main even manage and control it. On the contrary, wealth has become so great and so concentrated that as a matter of fact, it controls those who possess it.

About three-quarters of the wealth of this country is in corporate form, over one-half of it is under the domination of 200 corporations, which in turn are controlled by what Ferdinand Lundberg, in his recent book referred to as "America's Sixty Families."

Eight years ago America's sixty families had held in their hands, since the close of the World War, complete domination over the political life of this country. They had lulled the American people into the conviction that if the people would grant conditions in which these sixty families would put capital to work, enterprise would boom, wages would soar and there would be two cars in every garage.

The people gave the sixty families this confidence; gave the sixty families this trust in their benevolent despotism—in short, gave them then what they ask for today, and what happened? Out of their divinely claimed genius as managers of private enterprise, the sixty families promptly led the American people into the worst peace-time catastrophe ever known."

(New York Times, Dec. 31, 1937)

Certain basic lines of growth have been followed in the development of industry that created the wealth and power of the Morgan-Mellon-Rockefeller dynasty. In the days of our fathers small factories existed, employing a few wage-earners and using little capital. In the development of the industrial life of America these small factories gave place to larger and greater manufacturing institutions employing many hundreds of men with specialized high-speed assembly lines. The great capital investment required by the larger corporations of today forced out of existence the individually owned

227

businesses which employed a few people. With the growth of gigantic industrial units and corporations, the control of capital played an increasingly important part in our economy, and led to the development of great banking and industrial monopolies which drew out an ever-increasing share of the profits in the form of dividends, with a decreasing share going to the working class. Industrial interests developed banking properties, and banks gained control of corporations. A new form of banking developed, known as finance capital, giving the financier connections with the major banks concerned both with banking and industrial finance. Thus have monopoly, capitalism, and imperialism grown. They have been developing ever since the Civil War, and the process of concentration of capital into the hands of the few continues to accelerate.

Capitalism began its ascendency during the Civil War of 1861–65 * with the passing of chattel slavery. Prior to 1860 the total manufacturing facilities of the country were still small, and plants engaged in the processing of raw materials more numerous than those engaged in manufacturing. However, manufacturing was well on its way to rapid growth. Soon the sewing machine, farm machinery, machine tools, and manufacturing machinery made in the United States had gained a reputation as the world's best. In 1820 there were 349,000 small factories. In 1859 the number had decreased to 140,433, but the number of wage earners employed in manufacturing had grown to 1,300,000, and these workers were producing two billion dollars' worth of merchandise.

Manufacturing and mining expanded rapidly after

* The Morgan banking empire was founded in 1861.

228

the Civil War. The copper mines of Montana and Utah, the iron ranges of the Lake Superior country, and copper and iron mines in Michigan were developed. The manufacture of steel was multiplied by the discovery of the Bessemer process. As the country grew, the technological age came in, giving industry a new impetus. Manufacturing became concentrated into larger and larger units, the straight-line method of manufacturing and assembly was initiated by Henry Ford, and systems of production became more centralized and more mechanized.

In 1900 two-thirds of the total value of manufactured products were produced by corporations. A generation later, corporations were producing ninety instead of sixty-five per cent of our needs.

What are corporations?

Corporations are fictitious personalities created by law. In industry and banking the corporation is a device used to draw capital from many people who have a surplus, in order that their capital may be used to earn a profit for them in the shape of dividends. These investors take no active part in management, as a rule. When investing or buying stock in the corporation of today they lose all control over the money they have put into it, for the management is now handled by professional directors elected at the dictation, and acting under orders of the controlling bankers. At least eighty per cent of the wealth of the United States today is corporate wealth.

Banks play an ever-increasing part in the control of corporate wealth by means of their finance-capitalist arrangement. As industry aggregated into super corporations, the demand was created for huge investments. The industrialist was forced to go to the local bank, which turned to the larger New York banks for help. Thus the bankers came into a full knowledge of the industrialist's affairs and demanded the privilege of naming members of the Board of Directors. Through the advancing or withholding of capital, the banker was enabled either to assist or destroy a business. The battle a few years ago between Henry Ford and the New York bankers is legendary. Ford was enabled to escape the conspiracies of the bankers to gain control of his company through his ability to draw capital from his thousands of dealers throughout the country. Had Ford been unable to obtain funds from sources other than the banks, he would have had to sacrifice control of his empire as a price for bank finance.

While wage earners were walking the streets in the vain search for work, and wages were being cut throughout the country, dividend and interest payments rose from $1,865,000,000 in 1915 to $8,075,000,000 in 1931.

With the birth of the twentieth century, American capitalism took a new part in world affairs. The salient causes leading to this expansion were the exhaustion of free public lands; manufactured products replaced raw materials as the main exports of the United States; large corporations created monopolies in many lines; the major banks of the country accumulated an abundance of capital for investment, which led to their control of insurance and trust companies and the mechanism for floating new security issues.

When the United States found domestic expansion

slowing down with the passing of the frontier, monopoly capitalism sought new fields overseas, and entered into competition with the financiers of Europe. While Europe was engaged in war and borrowing billions from the United States, Wall Street built the greatest financial and political power in the capitalistic world.

This financial power is centered in Wall Street of New York City in a narrow, inner oligarchy comprised of the leaders of the strongest financial groups. Through their New York banks, they dictate to the smaller banks of the country and help them to a share of the spoils, subject always to destruction if their independence threatens the interests of their overlords.

The Rockefellers, Morgans, and Mellons are the three leading financial groups in the United States. These groups act together where their mutual interests are concerned, but in opposition in their struggle to attain the top of the financial pyramid.

The same forces that bred these financial empires, with their dictatorship over every basic industry and their world-wide contacts, also keep in play both competition and cooperation among the varied groups. Though rival financial groups may have investments in the same concern, you may be sure that below the smooth surface of cooperation, each is in opposition to the other in the war to gain greater power and privilege.

By the intermarriage of members of the great moneyed clans, the wealth of the country comes more and more into the hands of the sixty families, and so today, as in feudal society, it is the family that controls the banks and banking partnerships, and through them, the great corporations of the nation.

As the family in imperial Rome maintained its power in government, so do the sixty families, in no less degree, maintain their governance over wealth—accumulating it, guarding it, keeping it intact from generation to generation. The family is a sacred institution protected by custom. No agency of government can pry far into the secrets of a family. Therefore, we find the family-owned holding company strongly entrenched today, and their main concern and purpose is the concealment of money from the tax collector. The family provides protection above the law for financial skullduggery that could not be found either in a partnership or corporation.

ROCKEFELLER EMPIRE

It is impossible to conceive of the power of the Rockefeller millions. With assets of over twenty billions, theirs is the strongest influence in banks and corporations. Their real estate holdings are not included in this sum. The Rockefeller holdings also extend another twenty-four billion into concerns in which the Morgans have interests. The Standard Oil Company, with close to five billion in assets, is but one of their many holdings.

MORGAN EMPIRE

The Morgans control over thirty-five banks and insurance companies and sixty non-financial corporations. A known sixteen billion is but a small part of their assets in another group of sixteen banks and miscellaneous corporations. In fact, their gross assets total nearly one-sixth of the wealth of all the corporations of the nation, or about *one-seventh of the combined wealth of the nation.*

232

The Mellons are interested in some thirty-five banks, insurance companies, and forty or more non-financial institutions. Their combined assets are four and a quarter billion. They have additional interests of some twenty-six billion in corporations allied with the Morgans, Kuhn, Loeb & Co., and other bankers.

MINOR EMPIRES

Other families or groups controlling vast wealth are the Du Ponts, the banking firms of Lee, Higginson & Co., Kidder, Peabody & Company, Brown Brothers, Harriman Company, Lehman Brothers, and Goldman, Sachs & Company. It is reported that in one year the Du Ponts took some fifty million dollars in dividends out of General Motors Company, just one of the companies they control. For every dollar paid that year in wages by the General Motors Company, another dollar was paid in dividends.

These financial dictators are the real rulers of the United States, and by means of propaganda they control public opinion and, directly or indirectly, every action of the cabinet and legislative bodies of the nation. Their concentrated wealth is used to conceal and cover up their financial deals, and counteract public resentment of their methods. Some years ago, the elder Rockefeller was the most heartily hated man in the United States. He hired an outstanding publicity man who has managed, in a few short years, by judicious planting of stories all biased in Rockefeller's favor, to change the public's hate into profound respect, if not hero worship.

Destructive to the public good as are some of the

policies of the "economic royalists," the fact remains that they are essential to the evolution of the economy of the country. Were it not for the men with ability to build our mammoth corporations of today, there would be no training schools to develop the ability to operate efficiently the super-corporation of tomorrow, the corporate state foretold by Edward Bellamy.

The five methods used by our financial overlords to control public opinion are: the newspapers, radio, movies, philanthropies, and schools. The newspapers, most potent of the five in molding public thought, are given first consideration. It is a standing policy of our newspapers to defend, either directly or indirectly by implication, the actions and policies of entrenched privilege. The institution of journalism in the United States—the property of the multimillionaire families—is an efficient tool in building up a counter barrage against the progressive tendencies of the people.

The Radio Corporation of America is but one of the Rockefeller-Morgan-Mellon properties. This company builds or controls through licensing arrangements, eighty-five per cent of the broadcast receivers sold in the United States, and through its N. B. C. maintains a censorship over the information to reach the people over the air. Columbia Broadcasting Company is under the control of the Lehman Brothers, Brown Brothers, and Harriman banking groups, who see that no time shall be sold to any organization concerned with airing too much economic truth.

Eight major producers make sixty-five per cent of the pictures and control eighty per cent of the capital invested in the motion picture industry. All of the news reels are produced by this group. In the Twentieth Century set-up, there are over two hundred corporations—a financial puzzle that the government itself cannot penetrate. Far more difficult than guessing which of the three shells conceals the little pea is the task of tracing the profits through the maze of this complicated corporate structure. The subject matter of the news destined to reach the public, and that of the lessons implied in feature pictures, are all dictated in Wall Street, and not in Hollywood. The slaughtering of innocent people by the police of Chicago in the strikes of a few months ago should have been big news. Not one foot of film shot at the scene of action ever reached the theatre screen.

The universities and schools of the country are also dominated by this same group, and nowhere is class consciousness as strongly exhibited as in our colleges. By means of money grants and bequests given only to those schools whose curriculi contain little of a progressive nature, and the selection of trustees from the monied class, the education of the youth of the country is held within the narrow limits of capitalistic vision.

This is true not only of the schools and universities on the east coast, but also of those on the west. The president of one of the largest west coast banking groups has his fingers in many pies. No doubt he is a busy man.

According to the Stanford University Bulletin, March 31, 1939, Graduate School of Business, Mr. Teague is connected with the following:

President, Security First National Bank, Los Angeles.
President, California Fruit Growers Exchange.
Chairman, Santa Clara Water District (since 1927).

President, Ranco La Cuesta (since 1930).

Regent, University of California (since 1930).

President, Agricultural Council (which is virtually legislative arm of Associated Farmers, Inc.).

Vice-President, Institute of Cooperatives (since 1933).

President, California Walnut Growers Association (since 1912).

President, Limoneira Company (since 1917).

President, Thermal Belt Water Company, Santa Paula (since 1917).

Director, National Cooperative Council (since 1933).

President, State Chamber of Commerce (from 1932–34, was on Hoover's Farm Board, that arch-reactionary body, foe of small farmers).

The head of another leading California banking chain is largely interested in speculative farming. Both of these banks have interests in large agricultural corporations, and are fast developing a form of Fascism in California through their Associated Farmers' Corporation, which would have been more aptly titled "Associated Bankers and Industrialists."

By control of the people's money, one-fourth of which is deposited in eleven of the largest banks (seven in the East, two in Chicago, and two in California), Big Money can either finance or wreck any business institution. The government is not permitted by our bankers to enter any field of banking that can yield a profit. The banking service of the postal department is confined to such narrow limits that it has never been a threat to private banking. By means of generous contributions to both political parties, the ruling families obligate our officials so that they may later demand no legislation be passed that might prove destructive to their established privileges. By means of their contributions to campaign funds, the sixty families shape and control our laws. Should we elect a progressive president, they always

236

manage to tie his hands and sabotage his efforts by dictating who the members of his cabinet shall be and, through campaign contributions to reactionary congressmen, elect sufficient reactionaries to block progressive legislation.

At no time in recent history has the shortsightedness of Big Money been shown as in the past eight years. Every well-informed economist is aware that Roosevelt saved the banks for the bankers and probably postponed a revolution in the United States that would have liquidated the owning and banking class. Instead of permitting sufficient progressive legislation to be passed, which would in a small degree correct the causes of our economic breakdown, our sixty families have caused such a barrage of misinformation to be given the people that public opinion has turned from an appreciation of progress to fear of it. For twelve years, prior to Roosevelt, the bankers were given complete freedom to run the country as they saw fit. With their return to power they will force Fascism upon this country, an act which will, within a few years, bring about their own complete destruction.

The trend has been steadily towards concentration of wealth in the hands of the few. The rich are getting richer while the poor become poorer. The old saying: "From shirt-sleeves to shirt-sleeves in three generations" is no longer true, for by intermarriage of members of the sixty families, their wealth has increased to the point where no one can spend it. The great fortunes are forced to grow larger and larger, for the income is so immense that reinvestment is compulsory.

The Brookings Institute, a capitalistic-owned research

237

institution, reports that one-tenth of one per cent of the rich families receive an income equal to forty-two per cent of the families of the United States. Six million families, or twenty-one per cent, have incomes less than $1000.00 a year; twelve million families have incomes less than $1500.00; and twenty million, incomes of less than $2500.00. Only eight per cent, or two million families, have incomes of over $5000.00.

Living standards of the American worker have risen but little since the depths of the depression. The mounting cost of living gives the worker little chance to better his lot.

The recovery from depression was halted by deliberate sabotage on the part of our sixty families. The sit-down strikes of the workers received acres of publicity, but the sit-down strike of capital was ignored. Secretary Ickes gives an account of their policies:

To the 130,000,000 people of the United States the sixty families have made the threat that unless they are free of regulations to protect the people's money, unless they are free to accumulate through legal tricks, by means of corporations, without paying their share of taxes; unless they are free to dominate the rest of us without restrictions on their financial or economic power; unless they are once more free to do all these things, then the United States is to have its first general sit-down strike—not of labor—not of the American people—but of the sixty families and of the capital created by the whole American people, of which the sixty families have obtained control.

If the American people call this bluff, then the America that is to be free will be a democratic America, a free America.

If the American people yield to this bluff, then the America that is to be will be a big business, Fascist America—an enslaved America.
(New York Times, Dec. 31, 1937)

The 1940 presidential election will be the last under our present system. The executive elected in November

238

1940 will soon become a dictator of a fascist state although it will still be called a democracy.

"Capitalism is an intermediate stage—it could exist neither under conditions of complete scarcity nor complete abundance," says Walter B. Pitkin of Columbia University. True communism is a condition of abundance. Fascism is a condition of scarcity. Fascism is a counter-offensive instituted by the owning class, aimed at the maintenance of their power and privileges through the destruction of communism. Fascism is reaction armed to destroy progress. It is capitalism plus murder. It is atavistic, feudalistic, and a revival of paganism.

Fascism, hidden behind a false face of simon-pure Americanism, is still Fascism, and means the killing of the Bill of Rights and every liberty enjoyed by the American people. Fascism is in power in Washington, D. C. Vicious streams of propaganda are persuading the people of the United States that black is white. The same tactics are being followed here that proved successful in Italy and Germany.

In those countries socialism was the bait used to conceal the hook. In this country it is "Americanism," "Christianity," and the "Constitution,"—terms all acceptable to the average man—that hide the poison. This type of propaganda is extremely well organized and heavily financed. It has one aim—the mis-education of the American people. It is meeting with fearful and horrible success.

The United States was forced into the last war largely through the false leadership of the House of Morgan with the assistance of the sixty families. When England declared war on Germany in September, 1939, J. Pierpont Morgan was shooting grouse in Scotland with the King of England. As he got us into the first World War, so will he bend every effort to get us into the second. It is so much safer to get our people into an overseas war than to risk revolution at home. But nothing Morgan, or any other banker, can do will change the destiny of the United States.

Six thousand years ago Abraham led his people out of a country where the land was possessed by a few, and established a new order wherein there was plenty for all. Three thousand years later Moses reenacted the play. And now, in Kosmon, there will be a general exodus from limitation into peace and plenty. This world chaos means that the land will, once again, be returned to the people. Every bit of wealth there ever was, or ever will be, is the product of mother earth.

However, the owners of the land and factories, the source of the real wealth of the country, are not going to give their plunder back to the people without a struggle which will precipitate a civil war.

But wars have their redeeming features as well as their evils. Wars destroy the old and pave the way for new and better reconstruction.

In every apparent evil there is a seed of good. The men of initiative and brains who have developed our banks, corporations, and institutions have been well rewarded for the good things they have accomplished, and will suffer for every mistake they have made. Let us be thankful for them and recognize the marvelous work they have done rather than condemn and blame them.

It has only been by the concentration of wealth and

power in the hands of the few that our corporations have been built and the executive brains developed that will make possible the super-corporation of the state pictured in Bellamy's "Looking Backward," "Equality," and other books.

Russia, in its efforts to provide plenty for all of its people, had first to develop the factories to build the machines necessary for rapid production. Lacking the engineering brains and ability in their own country, they were forced to send to the United States for engineering talent. We are fortunate in having that talent trained and developed in the corporation schools, at present, owned by our sixty families. Some day this talent will be used to manage efficiently our productive units for the profit of all rather than for the profit of the few.

Today every city, county, and state statute book is filled with laws outgrown and unobserved. For years our people have been losing freedom, little by little, through laws adopted at the instigation of various pressure groups. Most of these laws are for the sole purpose of increasing the earnings, rights, and privileges of the group sponsoring these laws rather than for the good of the public. Our legislators seem unable or unwilling to revoke countless useless and detrimental laws, and each year load us down with thousands more, further restricting our freedom. History tells us that peoples of the past have regained their freedom by revolution. Prophecy informs us that our people will clear the decks for a new dispensation by means of a second civil war.

During its few remaining years capitalism in America will become Fascism. Freedom of speech and assembly, the Bill of Rights, the security of the home, and every other protection to American liberties will be temporarily destroyed by Fascists, dominated and financed by the sixty families and other large owners of the wealth of our country.

Such is the destiny of the United States, and none can change it. It will be the means of forcing our people to regain lost liberties and to step forth into a newer and larger freedom. Our partial freedom of the past must be sacrificed for a short time that we may learn to really appreciate freedom, to the end that the dawn of a new day may bring a new birth of freedom and economic liberty for all.

The years between 1914 and 1948 are thirty-three years marking the transition period from the Fascist government of today to the cooperative commonwealth of tomorrow. The United States of America in its early days was a government by the people for the people. In the years since 1776, as symbolized by the pyramid on the dollar bill, it has changed from a government of the many to a government of the few.

The space between the topmost layer of the pyramid and its capstone enclosing the All-seeing Eye of the Creator symbolizes the years between 1945 and 1948 when this country will be virtually without a government.

The mis-government of this over-rich few will precipitate a revolution that will return our nation to the democracy it was designed to be. The comparison between the government of today and that of tomorrow is shown in the parallel columns which follow:

The Un-United States of Today and the Re-United States of Tomorrow

From 1940 to 1948

PRESIDENT now a dictator. Supposed to be chosen by the people, but in reality selected by the HOUSE OF HAVE which gives the people a choice of two men either of which will represent big business and the bankers.

CONGRESS now elected for political ability and business connections rather than character and executive accomplishments. Trade votes to further passage of legislation favoring special interests.

SEMI-CORPORATE STATE that owns post office, harbors, rivers, and retains title to a few of the country's resources. Recognizes private ownership of corporations, farms, factories, and tools of production for private profit.

UNIONS are in constant conflict with owning class and between themselves. The A.F. of L. Unions are reactionary, unprogressive and capitalistic. They tend to Fascism, for they are governed by an executive board that has entrenched itself as dictator. A.F. of L. represents the small group of skilled mechanics.

1948 and After

PRESIDENT selected by the people, not for his political ability but for his spiritual and intellectual attainments. He will head the nation because he is the most able of any citizen to lead wisely and build constructively. He will be a beneficent ruler not a malevolent Fascist dictator.

CONGRESS will consist of a council of men selected for their outstanding ability in their various specialities. Council will advise the president, but he will make the decisions, thereby avoiding vote trading, etc.

CORPORATE STATE owning all natural resources, railroads, utilities, cooperative farms, factories, and tools of production and operating them for the greatest public benefit.

UNIONS are a thing of the past. Fraternities have taken their place. Each fraternity selects its most able member to represent it on the council. Chief of each council represents his council on the next higher council, thereby selecting the best men who form the National Council similar to the former cabinet.

243

C.I.O. is representative of the Communistic thought. They organize all employees in an industry rather than the few high paid workers. Both forms destroyed by dictator during war years.

ECONOMY as in all other countries during the last years of the War of Armageddon, planned only for war purposes. Over-production in the midst of starvation still persists.

ECONOMY planned for the most efficient use of tools of production and conservation of natural resources. Every citizen benefits from collective efficient operation and receives benefits comparable to $10,000 a year under the capitalist set-up.

EDUCATION controlled to a large degree by owning class. Freedom of the press, free speech and free assembly abolished. Individual may educate himself and reject the curriculum of the Fascists but he must keep silent or go to jail. Military training compulsory.

EDUCATION. Both brain and hand are trained. Youth receives scholastic training in school and practical experience in industry.

YOUTH is forced into military training camps or into industry engaged in manufacturing implements of war.

YOUTH is given the benefits of army discipline, but discipline is utilized for peace and not for war, which has been abolished.

YOUTH, at completion of schooling, is required to serve in peace army of general public service for three years. From the age of 18 to 21 both young men and women belong to groups similar to the C.C.C. and do similar public service work.

SCIENCE. The scientific mind is confined by the ortho-

SCIENCE is unhampered in its research to improve living

From 1940 to 1948

doxy of usury and the capitalistic system built upon it. Unlimited scientific research for additions to the products of the private profit system. Continual invention of machines which cause more unemployment, more deadly war machines, but inventions that would upset returns from investment of private capital are withheld or destroyed.

RELIGION. Religious liberty, provided in the constitution, invalidated by organized churchery. Fascist groups, organized to stir up religious hatred, succeed in establishing a fictitious Christianity as a state religion.

STANDARD OF LIVING has suffered during war years. At beginning of 1940, there were eleven million unemployed and twenty-five million without adequate income to insure a healthy diet. As rich grew richer the poor grew poorer until millions were slowly starving.

WAR between Japan and the U. S. A. followed by civil war between the Fascists and progressives.

1948 and After

standards, health, welfare of the people. Inventions are public property. Only the best are used that products manufactured may be most efficient, beautiful, and durable.

RELIGION is that of the Fatherhood of the Creator, the Motherhood of the Earth and Brotherhood of man. Religion of words has made way for a religion of works.

STANDARD OF LIVING is now the highest in the world's history. Every one now assured of plenty of all good things of life.

WAR, imperialism, aggression, and conflict have given way to peace and cooperation. All national barriers to free trade, travel, and emigration have disappeared.

CHAPTER XXI

The Writing on the Wall

Mene, Mene, Tekel, Upharsin!

MENE: God hath numbered thy kingdom and finished it.
TEKEL: Thou art weighed in the balance and found wanting.
UPHARSIN: Thy kingdom is divided and given to the Medes and Persians.

Three thousand years ago this warning flashed upon the wall where Belshazzar, King of Babylon, and his thousand nobles feasted.

Upon a thousand motion picture screens throughout the United States another warning is written. "Gone With the Wind" is a story of yesterday—and a prophecy of tomorrow.

Of all the reviews, criticisms, comments, and opinions written and voiced about this picture of a decade, we have yet to find one expressing a conception of the spiritual and prophetic import of this story.

A book selling two million copies (1,750,000 in the U. S. A.), resulted in a picture costing three million dollars, which returned the investment within the first eight weeks of its release. It has broken all records for the number of people reading the book and will, if the hundred million estimated audience see the picture, break all screen records.

An accident?

I think not.

Spiritual forces inspired the story and overshadowed every person who took a part in its telling.

To what purpose?

The warning is given to the rulers of today, as a warning was given Belshazzar and his nobles of another day.

Of the one hundred and thirty-five million people in the United States who read and saw the popular "Gone With the Wind," how many will receive the message it is aimed to convey?

Not many, and few indeed of those most concerned.

Belshazzar could not read his warning. The House of Have considers "Gone With the Wind" just another picture. The interpretation of the writing on the wall did not save Belshazzar, nor will this or any other interpretation of the meaning of this movie save the rulers of today from destruction.

It is a spiritually inspired message to those spiritually blind.

Eighty years ago the Creator's clock struck the hour for the destruction of chattel slavery on this American continent. Tomorrow the clock will strike again to mark the hour for the release of horse-power slaves and their wage-slave overseers from bondage to the few. They shall be released to provide plenty of nature's abundance for everyone, instead of profit for the owners of the land, mines, mills and factories.

Could the slavery and economic questions of eighty years ago have been peaceably settled?

I doubt it.

Many thinking people realized long before the Civil War that a condition was fast developing which could only end in trouble. In 1800 the richest parts of the

South had a slave population of fifty per cent. Forty years later the proportion of slaves had increased to seventy per cent. Another twenty years (1860) found ninety per cent of the population of these same areas in bondage.

A few who studied conditions of that day and sought a peaceful solution to the problem, advised the purchase of the slaves by the government at a fair price, and then advocated their release to freedom, believing that in this way slavery could be peaceably abolished.

Who resisted this solution?

The owners of the land to whom belonged the slaves upon it. These shortsighted owners would not consider such an "infringement of their rights." They loved the old economy, and would not admit that a new day was at hand. With all their combined selfishness, prejudices, passions and lust for power, they resisted change. By force of arms they resisted progress and the forward march of freedom. New and rigid laws were passed. It became unsafe for anyone in the South to voice an opinion that slavery was wrong, and that the abolishment of it would bring a new and better economy with more abundant life to slave owners as well as slaves. The forward thinking person of that day was labelled a nigger lover, a black hearted abolitionist, or a damned Yank, just as today's open minded student of world and economic conditions is being labelled a Red, a Communist, or an agitator, should he venture the statement that something is wrong with capitalism, or suggest that a more abundant life for everyone awaits the day when farms, factories and machines are freed to produce for all, instead of being withheld from production because they cannot produce a profit for the few owners in an economy based upon scarcity.

All the forces of church, press, finance and state were mobilized by land and slave owners to arouse the selfish sectional passions of the people of the South, and hate was whipped up for the abolitionists and people of the North.

They were willing to wreck and destroy the nation rather than free one slave.

They destroyed themselves, cost their country thousands of lives, and the nation a thousand times the number of dollars it would have taken to purchase and give peaceful emancipation to the slaves.

Strife and civil war, destruction, desolation and death resulted—and with it all they lost their slaves and wrecked the South for a generation. Half the country was left barren for the lifetime of those who wrecked it.

There is a powerful story in "Gone With the Wind," and a prophecy of tomorrow in terms of the past.

Rhett Butler, the Northerner, warned the rash young blades of the South, who gathered in the living room at Tara, of the disastrous results that would follow should the slave owners cause war. Men of small perspective and less vision could not visualize the power of the North, nor can our business men, bankers, industrialists and possessing classes visualize the power of an aroused, disposed populace. Keen observers are giving our reactionaries of today a warning similar to that given by Rhett Butler to his generation.

Mene, Mene, Tekel, Upharsin!

The revelers of a former cycle lacked the spiritual wisdom to interpret the writing on the wall. Even when interpreted for them by the prophet Daniel, the warning went unheeded.

Again the story is being enacted with a new cast.

Thinking minds today realize that an ever-increasing portion of our people are ill clad, ill fed and ill housed —if housed at all—in the richest nation the world has ever known. Millions are half starved, while food is destroyed in upholding an outmoded profit system. Nineteen and three quarter million inanimate horse power slaves are waiting to be released so that they may produce an abundance of everything for everyone!

In the old Bible the path of humanity for three thousand years was plotted for those who today have the spiritual insight to read the road map concealed in parable and allegory.

In the year 1881 the Creator inspired the writing of the Kosmon Revelations, and gave to those ready to accept it the one and only plan for a peaceful transition from the hell of competition into the peace of cooperation, mapping the way for a few pioneers to establish peace, plenty and security.

In 1887 Bellamy in *"Looking Backward"* painted a picture of the democratic, corporate state, with its economy of peace and plenty that will prevail in the year 1980 following the destruction of our present oligarchy of wealth.

For thirty years Upton Sinclair has been trying to educate the public to purchase through their government our utilities, land, banks, factories and machines from the stockholders of our corporations, so that they might be operated for the good and profit of all in place of a few. In all the pamphlets he has published there is some light given, and the subject is discussed in detail in his *"Letters to Judd," "The Way Out,"* and *"Your Million Dollars."*

In more recent years Technocracy, the Townsend Plan, End Poverty in California, Ham and Eggs, Mankind United, and many other movements have served to inform the public of the plenty waiting to become theirs when they are ready for it. Each of these plans aims at a peaceful cure of an economic cancer.

Who oppose?

The land and slave owners of today, the House of Have, the bankers, the rich industrialists, the sixty families, the Chamber of Commerce, and countless thousands who have a stake in the profit system. They will consider no other economy.

In December, 1931, in the early days of the depression, when the nation's millions of unemployed were walking the streets seeking non-existent jobs, the president of the Chamber of Commerce, Silas Strawn, took a vote among the various Chambers throughout the country on the following question, "Shall the United States government help the nation's desperate unemployed?"

197 voted yes.

2,534 voted no.

Thirteen to one against ANY attempt to relieve the situation, or any effort to find a solution to our economic crackup.

That was nine years ago.

Has their wisdom increased? Has there been a change in their state of mind? Have they any more vision today than they had nine years ago, or are they any more ready to contribute to a solution now than they were then?

Not in the least!

A wave of reaction has set in.

In California, Governor Olson's program for liberalized relief has been torpedoed and sunk. During a special session of the Legislature our elected representatives, at the instigation of the Chamber of Commerce, the Associated Farmers, banks, railroads, steamship companies and other reactionary groups sabotaged the plan for social reform, instituted a forty per cent cut in relief allowances affecting three hundred and seventy thousand clients, and fixed the monthly relief allowance at a maximum of fifty-eight dollars with resident requirements of three years instead of one. But the maximum is $58.00. Thousands are allowed only $26.65 a month for man, wife and two children, out of which they must pay rent, purchase food, medicines, clothes and all other necessities—an average of fourteen cents per day per person.

Single men and women receive $9.60 per month.

California is the fourth richest state in the union, and its relief allowances, though meager to the point of starvation, are far more liberal than many of the poorer states.

In the rich state of California the per capita income in 1939 was but $639.00, of which $132.42 or 20.8% were taxes. Those who work must contribute one fifth of their income to keep from starving the many whom our capitalists will not permit to work.

A report of the S. E. C. to the Monopoly Committee states that the twenty-six largest insurance companies have increased their holdings of farm land seven per cent in the last ten years. In 1938 their income from the sale of farm land had increased 900% in nine years— from $9,000,000 to $82,000,000. In 1938 insurance companies owned over a half billion dollars worth of farm real estate, and three quarters of a billion dollars in farm mortgages. The Department of Agriculture states that the insurance companies have a more aggressive foreclosure policy than any other class of farm mortgage holder. Profits on foreclosed farm land have been over $9,000,000.

Other huge profits are raked in annually in the form of 30% to 40% of the crops of tenant farmers. Glenn D. Rogers, an official of the Metropolitan Life Insurance Company, admitted that 1939 rentals, taken from the company's sharecroppers, amounted to $5,-000,000, and for the three years before that it had never fallen below $4,000,000 annually. He said that the company would make more money by operating farms on a share crop basis than by selling the huge tracts of farm land it has secured by foreclosures.

In 1939 the insurance companies made their usual billion dollar profit, or *three and a half million dollars a day*. Ten billions profit in ten depression years! While the companies were making their billion dollars profit, more than half of their full time agents, who were bringing in the business making this profit possible, were being paid less than $250.00 a year, according to a report of the Securities and Exchange Commission.

Enormous salaries at the top, starvation wages at the bottom!

A huge volume just issued by the National Industrial

Conference Board entitled, *"Enterprise and Social Progress,"* reveals that three-tenths of our population of the lower income groups are worse off now than at any time in the last thirty years.

At the same time the four richest groups are getting a larger share of the national income than ever before.

Every unbiased study of the evolution of capitalism reveals the same trends, the rich getting richer while the poor get poorer.

In the United States, the richest nation in the world's history, forty millions of our population are dependent upon payments from the government. Thirty million families have incomes of less than $750.00 a year, or about $2.00 a day. Three hundred and fifty thousand families, representing more than a million people, roam the land as itinerant farm workers.

The United States is a country having the resources and machinery to make possible a national income, in the year 1940, of one hundred seventy-five billion dollars, or approximately $4,500 per family. But these resources must be released for production instead of being kept in idleness because our business leaders can not operate them at a profit.

There is considerable difference in a family income of $2.00 a day—when you get it—and an income of $12.00 each and every day throughout the year. A difference in food and clothes and housing, in health and happiness.

The first is what we are getting under the capitalistic system of private profit based upon an economy of scarcity.

The second is what we will have under a system of cooperative mutualism, in which all the people of the nation will own the land, factories and electrical slaves.

In Brazil some estates are larger than the British Isles. In Chile five hundred families own over half the land. In the Argentine several families own over 150 square miles apiece, and in Bolivia and Peru twenty per cent of the population own ninety-nine per cent of the land. In California the land is no longer farmed by individuals who own their land, but by corporations who own and farm it. In the United States the Metropolitan Life Insurance Company owns more farms and more acreage than any other individual or corporation. Outside of Russia, it is the world's largest farmer. It farms its land through share cropping, or by employing the former owners of its farms at meagre salaries approaching peonage.

In England the nobility own the land, in Germany the Junkers, in Japan the Mikado is the richest industrialist and owns more acreage than any single individual or corporation. France had its two hundred banker-industrialist families who own and rule the country, and the U. S. A. has its sixty families.

When old Egypt died, four per cent of the people owned all the land.

When Babylon perished, three per cent of the people owned all the wealth.

When ancient Persia died, two per cent owned all the wealth.

When Rome fell, two thousand people owned the civilized world; and then followed the dark ages from which we did not recover until wealth was scattered or destroyed by continual wars.

> Ill fares the land, to hastening ills a prey,
> Where wealth accumulates and men decay.
> —Goldsmith

In the intermission between the first and second sessions of Europe's part in the War of Armageddon, Brazil, Peru, Ecuador, Bolivia, Argentina, Cuba, Chile and Mexico—almost fifty million persons on the American continents have been in revolt.

The year 1940 finds two-thirds of the earth's population living in nations at war. Three-fourths of the earth's surface is inhabited by people engaged in killing each other. China's 450,000,000 are fighting for life against 100,000,000 of Japan. The British Empire is made up of a half billion people of various races, many of whom are participating in (the Bank of) England's war. India, with its 350,000,000 will soon be engaged in a religious war.

The Plunder Bund is marching to war again and drafting the worker to fight its battles. War between the Have and the Have Not nations has been declared by the International Bankers with headquarters in the Bank of England. The wars in Europe and Asia are for no other purpose than to prevent plenty of the plenty for the common people.

Smothered under an avalanche of propaganda against the Communist and Fascist countries, the truth peeks out; there is no unemployment in the U. S. S. R., Germany, Italy and Japan. In the first three nations the state has absorbed and nationalized the banks. In China, soldiers of Japan are inoculated with Communist doctrine that will result in the destruction of the capitalism of Japan and the emperor worship that made it possible.

The U. S. S. R., the Communist sections of China and Mexico, are three places in which usury has been abol-

256

ished, and ownership of the land recovered by the people. Germany and Italy have absorbed corporations formerly owned privately and embodied them in the corporate state.

First monarchies, then republics, followed by cooperative commonwealths, these are the three steps in the evolution of government. Feudalism, capitalism, and common (governmental) ownership are parallel steps in the development of economics.

The capitalistic nations of the world fear the growth of the new economy which will eventually mean abundance for everyone, and these nations will soon gang up on the U. S. S. R. to destroy it if they can.

They will be as unsuccessful as the monarchies were in their efforts to prevent the evolution of the republican form of government.

The only thing that will prevent the United States from joining the "ganging up" will be our second civil war.

At a time when over ten millions are still unemployed, the President demands, at the behest of the reactionaries and owning classes, cuts of $477,000,000 for the W. P. A., $300,000,000 less for public works, $400,000,000 less of farm aid, and $60,000,000 from the C. C. C., totalling cuts of a billion and a quarter in relief . . . that the military budget may be increased $14,000,000,000.

A billion less for butter—$14,000,000,000 more for guns. Has he forgotten what he said at Atlanta in 1932? "The millions who are in want will not stand by silently forever while the things to satisfy their needs are within easy reach."

Is he unaware of what God, the chief executive of our planet, told our people in 1881?

I demand of thee that thou shalt give up thy army and navy. Is thy faith still more in weapons of death than in the voice of everlasting life? Esteemeth thou thy army and navy more to be depended on than thy Creator?

The 1914-1918 session of the war cost the people of the United States alone over eighty billion dollars. This is enough to:

Pay off all farm mortgages in the United States.

Build four schools at $250,000 each in every county in the United States.

Establish trust funds of $100 each for every blind and deaf person in the country.

Build four million modern homes including garage space and a new car fully paid for.

Give one member from each of five million families a round-the-world trip.

Enough money was spent on the first World War by the United States to accomplish, not one of the above, but ALL OF THEM.

The schools, the homes, the automobiles, the abundant life we might have had were dissipated in a war "to make the world safe for democracy."

It brought on world-wide unemployment, a ten-year depression in this country, and economic chaos. Instead of democracy, the harvest was the *destruction of freedom and democracy*, and an epidemic of dictators.

In the days of Julius Caesar it cost 75¢ to kill a soldier. By the time Napoleon came on the stage, the cost had increased to about $3,000 a man. In our Civil War the cost was $5,000 for every man killed, and in the World War of 1914–1918 the price was $21,000 for every one of the 8,358,315 soldiers killed—a total of 180 billion dollars!

Military experts estimate that the cost of killing a soldier in the present war is $50,000.

In the Japan-China undeclared war as many people were killed in two years as were killed in the four year World War.

How many are to be killed in Europe in the next seven years at $50,000 a head? The *first two weeks* of the blitzkrieg in France killed 500,000.

Roosevelt and Hull are following the path blazed by Wilson and Lansing. First: purchases of airplanes and munitions for cash as long as the cash holds out. Second: loans that will never be repaid. Loans to be spent in this country for articles of death; loans to be spent to kid the people of the United States that they are getting something of value for the man power, the energy, the oil, metal, timber and other natural resources that should be employed to relieve the starvation and suffering of our people, and to build them better homes and schools. Third: war.

Can all of the people be fooled all of the time?

For nine long years big business has sabotaged every effort to solve our economic problems. The year 1940 finds 10,000,000 men still out of work.

European nations solved their unemployment problems with rearmament and war. As the concluding chapters of this book are being written in the middle of August, 1940, it is evident that the United States is following the same bloody road to revolution.

First a barrage of lies, misrepresentation, war scare headlines in every conservative newspaper and magazine

259

in the country. Censorship of the press and radio in order to eliminate any article or broadcast that might give out the truth.

Forget the Constitution.

Skip the Bill of Rights.

Forbid the Communist party the ballot. Deport Harry Bridges. Pass a conscription law. Throw all labor leaders into the army where civil rights may be denied them and, if they talk too much, they may be court-martialed. Unconstitutional? Sure, but who cares?

Fascism-capitalism, plus murder.

Militarism, rearmament, storm troopers, dictatorship, concentration camps, an ever-lowering standard of living, while our resources are being dissipated in another banker's war.

Fifty million men in Europe either in the armies or working in industries engaged in supplying war materials. Soon, it is planned, our unemployed millions will be absorbed in similar activities.

But after the second armistice, *what?*

Can anyone using his powers of observation and reason not agree that the wars in Europe and Asia are but a prelude to a series of internal revolutions and civil wars similar to that of Russia after the first World War? Is it probable that the United States will abide in peace when the rest of the world is in chaos? Do not the signs of the times prove that the hour is near for the fulfillment of the prophecies of many seers and three of our former presidents, foretelling of a time of revolution and death in order that a new and better day may follow?

The nations of the world are lining up in two opposing camps. The people within those nations are dividing, now, into two schools of thought, just as our people did at the time of the first civil war when they separated into a group which opposed slavery and one which sanctioned it. The first Civil War is individualized in the character of Scarlett O'Hara, who asked but one thing of life—wealth. Every worthwhile thing in life was sacrificed to obtain it. The death of lifelong friends, the suffering and loss of thousands, the destruction of her South, meant nothing to her. Greed blinded her to everything but her own selfish ends. To obtain wealth, she married three men. Two were killed by the war and the third, Rhett Butler, left her with an empty universe in her hands when he abandoned her, supposedly to seek a better woman.

Capitalism, whore of Babylon, also has her three men, finance, church, and state. Like Scarlett's, two will be destroyed by the war. Finance, with its international system of exploitation built upon banker-controlled gold, is even now more dead than alive. The Church, with its billions of tax free property and its racketeering priesthood forever labelling "Forbidden" upon every progressive movement, will, as ever before, line up its forces on the side of reaction, and bless, in the name of God and the gentle Jesus, both sides and their implements of death, with the result that the peoples of the world will destroy all state-established and supported religions. The state will abandon capitalism, with its creed of much for the few and little for the many, in order to find a better mate in a cooperative economy of plenty for all.

The wars in Europe and Asia have brought Fascism to the United States. Fascism means a dictatorship by the House of Have, the death of every democratic liberty, of free speech, free assembly and the sanctity of the home. Fascism will precipitate a civil war and economic chaos.

The scenes of "Gone With the Wind" will be repeated on a national and more violent scale. Civil war, with the breakdown of governmental authority, marauding bands roaming the country seeking plunder and pelf, destruction of homes and industries, a people gone mad, are all scenes which will be repeated and reenacted from coast to coast and from Canada to Mexico.

By 1948 the present financial setup with its privately owned Federal Reserve system and member banks, our present form of money, our insurance companies, privately owned land, utilities, factories, and productive plants will be gone with the wind and be replaced by public ownership and a more equitable economy. Even our disunited forty-eight states will be supplanted by a new union of which each present state will be a united member.

Impossible, you say!

As impossible as the Russian Revolution, as impossible as the dismemberment of China, as out of the question as the conquest of Ethiopia and Albania, as improbable as the war in Spain, Poland, Finland, France and England . . . and just as certain.

If you had told the people of Spain or Poland that their country would soon be in ruins, if you had stated that their homes would soon be bombed, and their people in concentration camps, would they have believed you? Not any more than the people of our nation accept the predictions of tomorrow made by our economic prophets, forecasting a general crackup from an analysis of the ever-accelerating disintegration of our profit system, or prophecies herein contained based upon the scientific system of prophecy of the Essenes.

Is it an accident that all agree that the years from 1940 to 1948 are years of revolution, with the year between 1944 and 1945 the date of destiny for the United States?

Such sustained coincidence amounts to a law.

A study of many prophecies and the confirmation of their truth found in the countless signs of the times has convinced the writer that the nations of today will repeat the mistakes of the nations of yesterday. Change will come through war and revolution, and not through education as we wish it might.

The year 1948 will find present governments, state supported religions, the present financial and private profit system GONE WITH THE WIND.

At least four years of revolution and chaos are ahead.

What will YOU do in the meantime?

Three courses are open to you.

You may go along with the mob, blind to the obvious; you may side with the reactionaries in their attempt to make the world stand still; you may succumb to war hysteria and join the legions of hate; you may cling to a dying order and die with it; or you may step aside and let the stampede pass.

Should you be one of the few who are aware of the signs of the times and desire to move before the blitz-krieg comes, you may heed advice similar to that given by the statistician Roger Babson in a book copyrighted in 1937 and entitled *"If Inflation Comes"*:

Purchase a few fertile acres, well watered, located on some side road a few miles from a major highway. Bury a few drums of oil, cache a liberal supply of canned and dried food and other essentials which would be hard to obtain in the event that agriculture, manufacturing and distribution break down.

Use your money for the welfare of yourself and others rather than hoard it, for money may soon lose most of its purchasing power through inflation.

If you are of the small minority of spiritually minded, cooperative individuals comprising the builders rather than the destroyers, desiring no part in war or any activity pertaining to war, death and destruction; if you recognize the advantage of community rather than individual effort; if you desire to provide a way in association with others of like mind and development, our advice is to join one of the several colonies devoted to blazing the new way of life with peace, plenty and security for all in place of too much for the few and little for the many.

This is not

THE END

It is only the beginning.

OLD KING LABOR

I am old King Labor. I was cast asleep in the Garden of Eden.

I have been sleeping for ages, performing my work in a somnambulistic state. I am now awakening from my long sleep—I am *thinking*.

I have done all the work of the world since man first inhabited the earth.

I have made all the useful and beautiful things possessed by all mankind.

I have made all the inventions possible that are being used all over the world.

I have made all the vehicles that travel on land, water and in the air.

I have made all infernal machines that are now being used to kill my children.

I have fought all wars for kings and rulers and have paid all debts.

I have sunken great shafts into the earth and brought forth untold wealth for a greedy selfish few.

I have never done much real thinking—toiled from early dawn, till late at night.

Because of my long sleep the world has gone mad on war, and this has driven me to serious thought.

Now that I am thinking, a new force is being put into action.

I am doing everything in this world for freedom for all.

I am fighting the battles. I am feeding the world and paying all debts. I have never thought in war times before.

As a result of my thinking, monarchial governments and kingdoms are changing and bowing to my command.

I will see that they obey when this great war is at an end.

I have found out that I am the most powerful of all kings.

I have found I can and must rule all nations of the world.

I am the foundation upon which all good, useful and necessary things must rest.

The people cannot live without me.

This awful condition of mankind has caused me to think of all the miseries of my people.

And this is the greatest discovery of all ages, and will bring justice to all mankind. I am breaking the chains of dogmas and superstitions. All forms of unjust government must pass away.

I will control all that I have produced, that my children may be happy.

I will convert all implements of war into useful machinery for my people. And there shall be no more war and bloodshed.

I will shorten the days of labor, that my people may have more time for learning and pleasure.

I will make conditions impossible for millionaires and paupers to exist in the world. All food speculators, trusts and money monarchs must go at my command.

I will abolish all rules of tyranny from the domains of the earth.

I will not forget the past.

I am going to keep on thinking, working, enjoying life and making conditions more perfect, remembering all nationalities are my brothers and sisters, that the world is my country, doing good my religion, with liberty, happiness and plenty for all FOREVER.

OAHSPE
A NEW BIBLE

is the

WONDER BOOK OF THE AGES

Given to the world in the year 1881 this wonder book is a miracle of the Nineteenth Century. OAHSPE is a revelation of the new era. It contains the answer to every economic, social, spiritual and philosophical question in the minds of men. It is a history of our planet since its nebulous days, a record of the human race since its birth upon earth, a history of every major religion; and a *roadmap to health, happiness and security for the individual.*

If you would know of the origin and destiny of man, the cosmic causes and purpose of this "Time of Trouble" and of the "Heaven on Earth" that will follow, you should read OAHSPE for it is the key to the past, enlightenment for today and a prophecy for tomorrow.

A new unabridged deluxe edition of OAHSPE, a volume containing thirty-six books and a thousand pages, printed from the original Newbrough plates, will be released in March.

The first edition of OAHSPE sold for $7.50. Long out of print used copies have commanded from twenty to one hundred dollars. You may have a copy of the New Deluxe large print OAHSPE for $5.00 postpaid.

Order direct from

THE BOOK OF GOLD

152 West 42nd Street
NEW YORK, N. Y.

Descriptive Literature on Request.

Bibliography

Title	Publisher	Address
Archives of the Essenes of Kosmon		Los Angeles, Calif.
Armageddon Is at the Doors	Out of Print	
Baha'u'llah and the New Era	Bahai Publishing Committee	New York, N. Y.
Common Sense Magazine	315 Fourth Ave.	New York, N. Y.
Capitalism (Lecture Outline)	Haldeman-Julius Publications	Girard, Kansas
Changing Governments	Foreign Policy Association	New York, N. Y.
Destiny of the United States	Prophetic Age	Akron, Ohio
Daniel and Revelation	Out of Print	
Economic Consequences of the New Deal	Harcourt, Brace & Co.	New York, N. Y.
Factories in the Field	Little Brown Co.	Boston, Mass.
Hitler Is No Fool	Modern Age Books	New York, N. Y.
Intellectual Development of Europe	Out of Print	
Joanna Southcott	Camelot Press	London, England
King James Bible		
Kosmon Revelations	Essenes of Kosmon	Los Angeles, Calif.
Looking Backward	Houghton Mifflin Co.	New York, N. Y.
Letters to Judd	Upton Sinclair	Pasadena, Calif.
Mein Kampf	Adolf Hitler	Germany
Noted Prophecies	Out of Print	
Oahspe	The Kosmon Press	Los Angeles, Calif.
Our Country, Our People and Theirs	Macmillan Co.	New York, N. Y.

PROPHECIES OF GREAT WORLD CHANGES	Aquarian Ministry	Santa Barbara, Calif.
RUSSIA WITHOUT ILLUSIONS	Modern Age Books	New York, N. Y.
THE PRESENT WORLD CRISIS	Out of Print	
THE STRUCTURE OF THE AMERICAN ECONOMY	U. S. Govt. Printing Office	Washington, D. C.
THE NEW INQUISITION	Modern Age Books	New York, N. Y.
THE ANCIENT LOWLY	Charles H. Kerr & Co.	Chicago, Ill.
WHAT IS COMING?	Out of Print	